Praise for *The EduProtocol Field Guide, Book 2*

"I love the concept that EduProtocols are open pedagogy. The beauty of EduProtocols as lesson design frames is that students and teachers become familiar with the steps, yet they are flexible enough to allow for use with a variety of content. EduProtocols are the 21st-century innovation for instructional strategy."

—**Michael R. McCormick**, superintendent, Val Verde USD

"What teacher doesn't want to save time *and* teach better? In book 2 of *The EduProtocol Field Guide*, Marlena Hebern and Jon Corippo provide even more low-prep, high-return activities you can use tomorrow. They're nutritious—chock full of pedagogy and sound teaching practices. And they're also delicious—fun activities your students will beg for!"

—**Matt Miller,** author, *Ditch That Textbook*

"This past year, EduProtocols helped me find freedom from the lesson planning island. The idea behind these protocols is simple—they're student-centered lesson frames that can be used week to week that incorporate the 4 C's (critical thinking, creating, collaborating, and communicating) and provide a fifth C for students—consistency. By using them, I have seen an increase in student engagement and learning even while I decreased my amount of time planning. As a result, I have earned back cherished learning hours in class and family hours at home."

—**Adam Moler,** Social Studies teacher, New Richmond Middle School

"If there was an engagement-level gauging meter, the meter would swing to 110% when EduProtocols are being implemented in the classroom. Marlena Hebern and Jon Corippo have created a game changer with several low-level, high-ceiling protocols. They are not only transforming the way content is accessed by the students, but they are also changing educators' mindsets. As a new-to-the-middle-school ELA teacher, I could easily adapt any of the protocols to meet the diverse needs of my students in an inclusive classroom. It is one of the best inclusive practices! Both *EduProtocols 1* and *2* should have a place on every teacher's desk and be reread periodically to remind us that there is a better way to engage and challenge all students! This book is a timely reminder that we should teach better, give more instant feedback, and work more efficiently."

—**Nupur Sethi,** middle school English teacher

"*The EduProtocol Field Guides* distill best practices down to a do-able approach. Going straight to the heart of helping students learn in an engaging way, the authors gently offer insights on what should be happening in everyone's class with collaboration, choice, voice, and confidence-building content mastery. Rather than banging a teacher over the head with current research, citations, and edu-jargon and then page after page of deadly boring verbiage, they provide a friendly voice,a voice that asks "What are the essentials that a student needs to master academics in a fun and engaging way?" They interject enough humor that even a cynical, burned-out teacher could be brought back to life.

"These guides are definitely a must-have for teachers that want to burn their over-bloated teacher guides, get their life back from hours of meaningless grading, and move beyond unfocused classroom technology convenience tools.

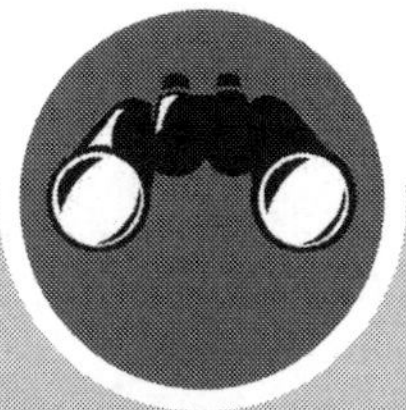

A Note from the Authors . . .

I am enough of an artist to draw freely upon my imagination.

—Albert Einstein

We wrote *The EduProtocol Field Guide, Book One* in response to our observations and experiences with teachers. We found that many were in search of tech-based alternatives that would engage students with relevant curriculum that embodied the Four Cs: communication, collaboration, critical thinking, and creativity. This book, Book Two, continues to develop the work we started in Book One. Some of the protocols gathered here are our originals, and others are iterations shared with us by teachers who read Book One.

As with our first book, the message of this book is a joint effort, a collaboration between us, Jon Corippo and Marlena Hebern, and some of the many educators we have come to know and respect. As we share personal stories and experiences, we will identify the speaker, but most of the time, you will hear a united voice as we explain the power and simplicity of the EduProtocols we've created and adapted. We hope you find it to be valuable.

We love to hear what other teachers are doing and hope you'll share your progress, ideas, and the lessons you create!

Connect with us on Twitter @mhebern and @jcorippo

Visit our website at EduProtocols.com

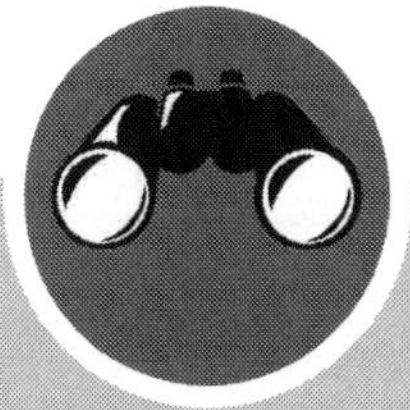

How to **Read This Book**

This guidebook may be read cover to cover, or you may access just the sections you need the most.

If you have not read Book One, *The EduProtocol Field Guide: 16 Lesson Frames for Infinite Learning Possibilities*, we strongly recommend that you do. It sets the stage for getting started with EduProtocols, presents the mindset for using them, and explains how to begin building a culture in your classroom to support the use of EduProtocols.

In this book, Book Two, we will review key ideas, continue to build upon the concepts developed in Book One, and share twelve newly developed EduProtocols along with nine teacher-reimagined iterations of protocols introduced in Book One. We will also explain the research-supported learning theories that are the foundation of the protocols and explain how Universal Design for Learning (UDL) and EduProtocols work together to support all learners.

We hope you will enjoy this second book and engage with us on Twitter using the hashtag #EduProtocols as you explore and expand your use of the EduProtocols!

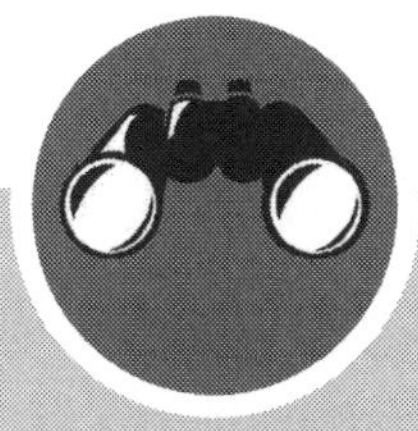

A Note on **Technology Platforms**

We use more than one platform to facilitate student collaboration. When we design for kids, we generally use Google, but Microsoft and Apple have developed collaboration features in their programs as well. Even though we originally designed them in Google, the activities in this book can be used on any platform that allows for collaboration. We won't get into the specifics of the programs we use in this book, so please refer to your own platform support to learn how to use its collaboration features.

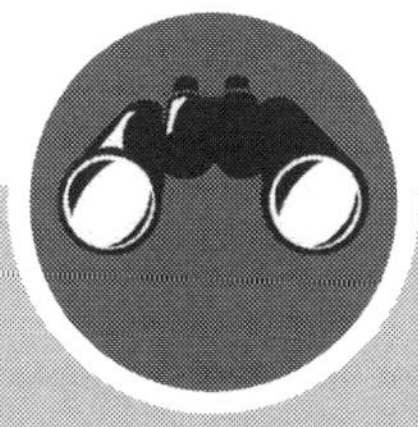

English Language **Learner Tip Box**

We have included tips for English Language Learners (ELLs) in the sidebars to assist you with providing support to students learning or struggling with English. These tips were contributed by our good friend Efraín Tovar, MAEd. Efraín is a California state–certified bilingual teacher and currently serves as a site leader-teacher at a middle school in California. He is the only U.S. multi-lingual, Google for Education Certified Innovator, Trainer, and Administrator who teaches English Language Development to students who are new to the United States. He is a regular speaker at local, state, national, and international conferences, where he teaches how to utilize technology to meet the linguistic/digital needs of second-language learners and their parents. He is the founder of @CAellchat, a global Professional Learning Network for teachers who teach second-language learners. Efraín serves on the Central Valley Computer Using Educators (@CVCUE) Board. You can follow him on Twitter @efraintovarjr.

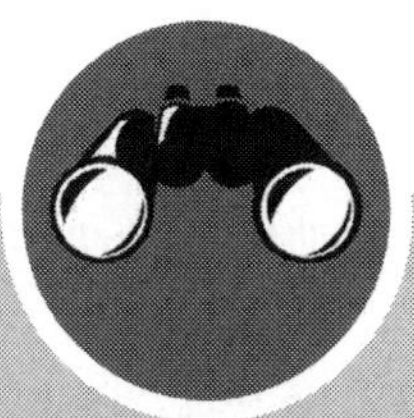

Foreword

Every once in a while, Providence brings together two things that are different, yet so complementary that the whole becomes greater than the sum of its parts. Better together—like Lennon and McCartney, or chocolate and peanut butter (I can hear Jon Corippo whispering in my ear, "Bacon and *anything*!"). I had the good fortune of meeting Marlena Heburn and Jon Corippo less a year ago, but almost instantly it seemed that we were pedagogical siblings of a common spirit. I had just introduced the T3 Framework for Innovation and they had just completed the *EduProtocols Field Guide One*, the prequel to the book you are now reading. We were all struck by how the T3 strategies for enhancing student voice, choice, and agency with digital tools were exemplified by the EduProtocol lesson frames.

I consider myself a researcher and a practitioner; in fact, I think we all should. The logic of the scientist is made far more experiential and appealing when rendered by the sensibilities of the artist. High quality educational research shows us that it's important to provide students with clear learning intentions, tightly aligned instructional strategies and learning activities, and ample feedback experiences. These elements should be seen as the building blocks of effective teaching and learning. Moreover, the classroom context also matters greatly, and so it's equally important to choreograph classroom interactions in such a way that enhances students' social and emotional development. So how can one teacher manage all of this by her or himself?

On this point, the research is also abundantly clear: Get the kiddos more involved! Inviting students to be more involved in collaboratively planning for their learning, creatively expressing and representing their understanding, and contributively monitoring and tracking their knowledge growth not only works, but serves to build students' collective voice, choice, and agency. This is the where the EduProtocols beautifully align the science of research with the artistry and serendipity of everyday classroom teaching.

To be sure, EduProtocols are not just activities designed to save time or engage students momentarily. Rather, they are a series of metacognitive scaffolds, or "Meta-Scaffolds." By that I mean that the EduProtocols are a collection of highly effective guides that help students develop metacognitive constructs through cycles of reciprocal creation, expression, and reflection. The EduProtocols, as you will see in this book, are also highly adaptable and can be implemented in any classroom, regardless of grade level or content area.

We learn better together than we do in isolation. It is through contribution that one experiences the power of harmonious human interaction. Implementing the EduProtocols with the guidance provided by the T3 Framework has the power to shift our classrooms more quickly from competitive learning spaces to contributive learning spaces. Over time, this will help to shift students' consciousness from the individual to the collective—from *me* to *we*. Research and action. Action and research. EduProtocols and T3. Better together.

—Dr. Sonny Magana
founder/CEO, Magana Education
Oxford Research Encyclopedia Scholar
Marzano Research Associate
author, *Disruptive Classroom Technologies: A Framework for Innovation in Education*

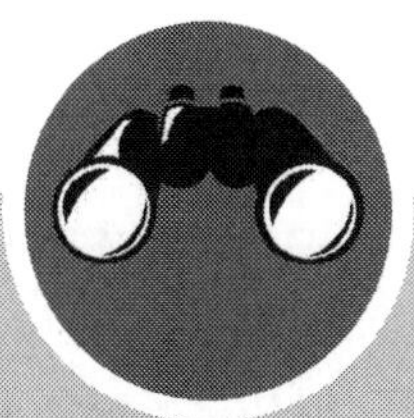

Foreword

We are years into the twenty-first century. Learning is different. Although many of the structures of school may seem the same, I challenge you to look closer. The way students can take opportunities to show their learning, its depth, and its complexity are in many ways very different from anything we may have experienced as learners.

When I was in middle school, our final project for eighth-grade history was a biography report. I was assigned John F. Kennedy. I went to the library, checked out three books about him, and hand wrote my paper—no images, no videos, no links to any outside sources. The only other person who read my report was my teacher. It was required to include a handwritten bibliography, which dropped my final grade to a B because of points deducted for misplaced commas. That was our big final project. I turned it in, and it was graded and returned, only to be thrown away since it didn't really matter.

I was working with a seventh-grade class recently. They were doing a research project (bit.ly/goodideahd) and had access to Chromebooks. The project asked that they review a series of good ideas on a playlist of videos (bit.ly/GoodIdeaPlaylistHD) to learn how big and small issues people face around the world are being solved by a variety of solutions from people of all ages. The students had the opportunity to choose a topic they were interested in learning more about, and they were taught how to navigate online research through identifying the credibility of the sites they found about the topic. They created dynamic websites (bit.ly/GoodIdeaReflectHD) showcasing their "reports" to educate each other about their topics for the next phase, their Good Idea Projects. The experience students had creating content to build understanding for their big class project was light-years away from my school experience. From the project's depth and complexity, to the blend of tech and analog tools, to the important application of the final project, students were learning content standards without the worksheets, without the lecture—and the results were astounding.

As teachers, we are tasked with getting our students career and college ready. Our schools have the opportunity and obligation to deliver relevant instruction that prepares students for what they will face beyond our classrooms. This is a learning process for kids, parents, and teachers. Just as we learned to read and write over time, learning in a technology-infused environment involves alternating between pen and paper, handheld devices, and laptops. The exciting part is that with this obligation comes the amazing opportunities that technology now affords us. We are able to connect, collaborate, create, and think critically with others well beyond the four walls of the classroom, effectively changing everything in terms of what is possible for learning in this modern world. But how do we accomplish this?

Jon Corippo and Marlena Hebern have the answer. Their first book, *The EduProtocol Field Guide*, has become required reading for the active learning classroom, supplying concrete solutions to accomplish-ing meaningful learning experiences. Their experience and insight into the way students learn, engage, and retain information is the basis for multiple bite-sized strategies that shift the way instruc-tion is delivered and elevates learning for students. With this new collection of EduProtocols, they take you to the next level with more ideas to change up the way you've always done things. The EduProtocols, while based on research, are clever, engaging, and easy to implement without hours of professional development; all you need is this Field Guide. This is the secret sauce to the work Jon and Marlena are doing; rather than writing a book about all the ways you should improve your teaching, they hand over a complete guide with solutions for how to make that happen. I'm excited for what you are about to experience as a teacher as you read this book, but really, I'm more excited for your students and the new learning experiences they will have in an EduProtocols classroom.

—Lisa Highfill
teacher, instructional coach
coauthor of *The HyperDoc Handbook*

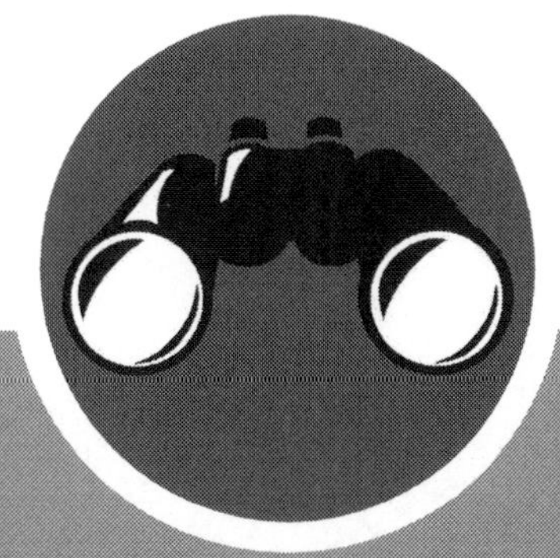

SECTION 1

A Field Glass Perspective

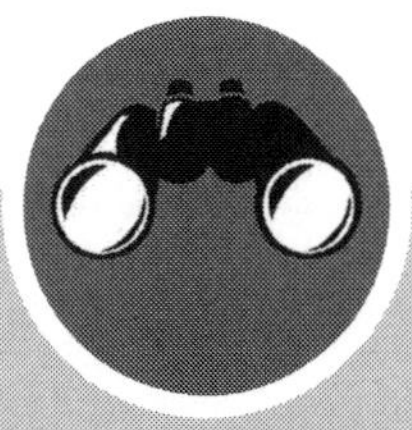

Chapter 1
What's the Rush?

We think children ought to learn while they're having fun.

—Hiroshi Yamauchi

The pressure to engage kids in meaningful, engaging, and enduring educational learning is growing as educators begin to see the impact that evolving technology is having on our students. Understanding this impact is the first step to addressing problems in our systems.

Technology is changing the world. In 2018 China's State Council committed to developing a $150 billion artificial intelligence (AI) industry by 2030. In June of the same year, a Chinese AI system beat fifteen elite doctors in diagnosing tumors. Scientists project that machines could take 50 percent of existing jobs by 2050, meaning that when our primary-aged students hit the job market, the shift will already be well under way. Kai-Fu Lee, founder of venture capital firm Sinovation Ventures and a top voice on tech in China, provides a little insight into what that future might hold. In a report by CNBC, Lee describes AI as *"the decision engine that will* ***replace people****."*

> **Jon**
> "The decision engine that will replace people"? *The very idea should horrify us!*

As we move toward an AI-infused society, automation of routine and non-routine human tasks will become the norm. When this automation becomes mainstream, it will be called the Fifth Industrial Revolution.

You have probably heard of the Industrial Revolution that took place between the eighteenth and nineteenth centuries and was the origin of the manufacturing process and mindset. Prior to this time, each household manufactured the things they needed by hand and with small tools. Then one day Sir Richard Arkwright of England invented a game changer: an automated spinning machine that sped up the process of making cloth. This early manufacturing device used water as an energy source and allowed merchants to quickly turn raw cotton and wool into cloth on a massive scale, replacing the tedious handweaving process.

Looking at the developments that occurred in the First through Fifth Industrial Revolutions can help us understand the historical impact of each time period as well as implications for our future.

Marlena

As you read this section, think about the shifts that are taking place in the world now and what they will mean for today's kids.

First Industrial Revolution

- 1760–1840
- The invention of manufacturing processes as envisioned by Sir Richard Arkwright

Second Industrial Revolution

- 1870–1914
- The automation of manufacturing and production lines were made possible using using electricity, steel, and oil (Thanks to Todd Rose in *The End of Average,* this is known as *Taylorism.*)
- Examples: Steel manufacturing, Ford Motor Company, development of the railroad

Third Industrial Revolution

- The 1950s and ongoing
- Movement from analog to digital along with the development and use of the computer
- Examples: The shift from cassette tapes (analog) to CDs (digital) to music files that you download from sources like iTunes (digital); McDonald's kiosk ordering system with tableside food delivery

Fourth Industrial Revolution

- Now!
- Development of new technologies such as robotics, nanotechnology, quantum computing, biotechnology, The Internet of Things (IoT), 3-D printing, and autonomous vehicles
- Examples: Nanotechnology house paint, your Google Home or Amazon Echo that can control your home camera and house temperature, and on-demand 3-D-printed materials such as those created on the space station (e.g., the first space wrench was printed in 2014)

Fifth Industrial Revolution

- Beginning now and fully emerging sometime in the future
- The development and use of AI in the automation of everyday tasks and manufacturing
- Examples: AI doctors, self-driving cars, financial management, service providers

Kai-Fu Lee has called the impending technological revolution the "singular thing that will be larger than all of human tech revolutions added together, including electricity, [the] industrial revolution, internet, mobile internet—because AI is pervasive." We can't help but wonder what a fully automated world will look like. We wonder what we will be doing and what jobs people will have. Japan is now considering the moral dilemma of blending AI with weaponry. Are other countries and scientists also considering the ethical questions associated with AI? Or will the future be more like Kahn Academy's founder Sal Kahn's vision of a society of creative artists? Most importantly for those of us who are teachers, how do we go about teaching a generation destined to be making decisions for this future?

Too Many Classrooms

Jon

I had the *exact same experience* at a totally separate time and place! Kids are fed so many options that they end up overwhelmed by them.

Marlena

Wait! Whatever happened to the moving sidewalks on every street? We were sure moving sidewalks would be a thing by now.

Jon

We are no better today at imagining the jobs or pathway of the future than we were in the 70s and 80s, but it doesn't matter; whatever happens, we have a pretty good idea that the world will be a different place.

Marlena walked into a classroom to assist a teacher one sunny fall day, and hanging on the wall, above the brightly lit windows, were fifteen graphic organizers. She looked down at the students, and sure enough, they each had a photocopied graphic organizer on their desk. One second grader (yes, you heard that correctly—a second grader) raised his hand and asked, "Teacher, what do I do now?"

Marlena suspected there was a new graphic organizer introduced every day, and that little second grader would ask that same question every time! Marlena sighed deeply and wondered, "How is a merry-go-round system of graphic organizers going to prepare these second graders for a fully automated AI future that we can barely imagine today?"

What skills will these students need to carry them into the Fourth and Fifth Revolutions? Is our idea of what these Revolutions will look like even accurate? The future we envisioned in the 1980s did not materialize as we imagined it would, and we know that thirty years out, innovations of the day will develop in similarly unexpected ways.

English Language Learner Tip: *Graphic organizers can be useful for ELLs to break down the flow of information, but only if the graphic organizer is used enough for the structure to become familiar to the student.*

Arwa Mahdawi speculates in *The Guardian* that three job categories will survive into the Fifth Revolution: jobs requiring genuine creativity (such as artists and scientists), jobs requiring complex relationships, and jobs that are highly unpredictable.

We need to consider how we are going to teach students the skills that will endure into the future, such as analyzing, comparing, evaluating, weighing options, defending, supporting, citing evidence, agile thinking, designing, communicating, and creating. Creativity must move beyond the maker space and into the mindset of every student and in every career opportunity. Is a graphic organizer reduced to a worksheet going to serve that purpose in the long run?

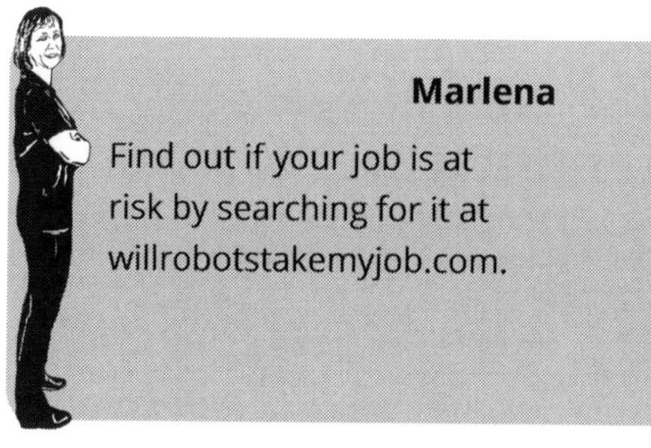

Marlena
Find out if your job is at risk by searching for it at willrobotstakemyjob.com.

On February 21, 2018, following a school shooting that took seventeen innocent lives, the Marjory Stoneman Douglas students stood in front of Senator Marco Rubio and the National Rifle Association spokesperson, Dana Loesch, at the nationally televised CNN Town Hall and defended their viewpoints on gun control and assault-style weapons. They did not have photocopied graphic organizers in front of them. Instead, these teenagers stood unfazed in front of their peers and the nation and debated the issue of gun control with adults who were seasoned in the art of debate and public speaking. At some point in their young lives, the Stoneman students had learned to defend and support their point of view, express themselves clearly, and cite the evidence needed to make a point.

Marlena
No one is going to hand out a stack of graphic organizers to our graduates and say, "Here. Now go make a difference."

When Emma Gonzales, a senior who survived the shooting, took the microphone at the town hall meeting, she said, "I want to thank Mr. Foster for teaching us everything we learned." At one point in the exchange, she turned to the noisy audience and shouted, "If I can't hear her statement, I can't come up with a rebuttal."

These students were using the skills they learned in school to stand before a national audience, a senator, and a spokesperson of the NRA to make their voices heard. Were they perfect? No. Were they well versed in their efforts? By all means, yes!

They had learned to make sense of the world around them, form and defend their point of view, and consider creative solutions to the problems they face. Isn't that what we want our kids to do?

How about Programs?

Imagine a teacher stopping Jon in the hallway and asking him, "Dude, do you have any new programs I could use? I need programs. I'm sure you know some really good ones for me."

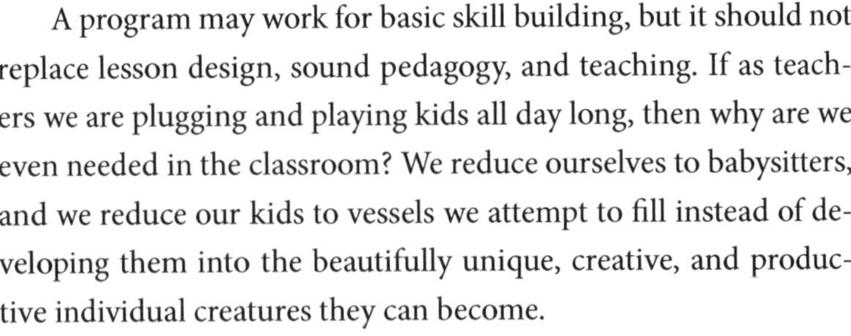

A program may work for basic skill building, but it should not replace lesson design, sound pedagogy, and teaching. If as teachers we are plugging and playing kids all day long, then why are we even needed in the classroom? We reduce ourselves to babysitters, and we reduce our kids to vessels we attempt to fill instead of developing them into the beautifully unique, creative, and productive individual creatures they can become.

> **Marlena**
>
> Teaching, if done right, is a complex job that we do not foresee shifting to automation. And the time to prove it is right now!

Plugging kids into a program with a set of headphones may help them learn some basic skills. Even adaptive learning programs are still skill-based programs with plugged-in students, and they allow someone in the district office to neatly track learning hours, gains in skills, and teacher use. (Marlena knows—she was lucky enough to have that job once.) Sure, graphic organizers have a place, and programs have a benefit, but to produce agile thinkers who are comfortable discussing and defending, quick responders, and most importantly, creative producers and contributers, we must go beyond the confines of corporately published curriculum.

What Is the Better Way?

The better way is anything that teaches students the transferable skills that will stand the test of time and help them understand the world.

> **Jon**
>
> We want to free up teachers and give them enough mental reserve to be able to dive into other skills, like computer science and project-based experiences..

EduProtocols are one way to do that. EduProtocols are lesson frames that can be used with any curriculum and are designed to allow students to engage in discussions, practice thinking with agility, and develop creativity as they show what they know. They are tools for teachers to use in their curriculum to teach skills, thinking, and content, and they are most effective when combined with other EduProtocols, lessons, or tools to deepen learning. They can be adapted to fit the needs of a particular classroom, learning situation, topic of study, or student in need, and they can be used to support a Universal Design for Learning (UDL) environment. EduProtocols act as the glue that carries the curriculum from one day to the next, and they leave time for other projects and class activities.

The first time we visited Chicago, we were amazed with the famous and delicious deep-dish pizza. Oh, what a delight! When we returned home to California, we learned that California pizza was a thing as well, with flavors like the BBQ Chicken Pizza made famous by the California Pizza Kitchen. We had taken these flavors for granted; they didn't seem that special to us. We later learned that New York pizza was well known in its own right. And Chicago cuts its thin crust pizza into squares! Even Saint Louis has a special regional recipe with Provel cheese made from cheddar, mozzarella, and provolone. Different flavors, but we still call them pizzas. The basic ingredients are the same: a crust made primarily from flour, yeast, and water, with sauce, cheese, and meat or vegetable toppings. EduProtocols are like pizzas: the same basic ingredients, but with endless variations!

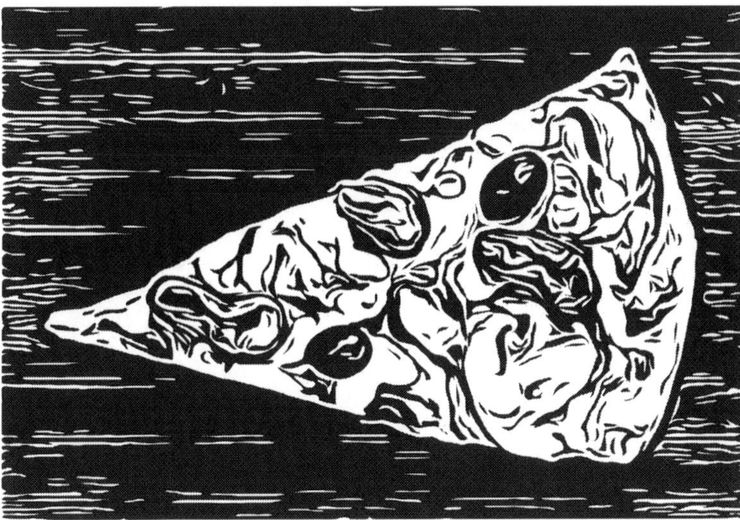

Jon

School is like a gas station hot dog. Gas stations don't know there are chili cheese dogs or Polish dogs or Chicago dogs out there.

Marlena

Just those same darn hot dogs on rollers.

Jon

Every school thinks its books and lesson plans are the best, but they are all just the same plain, roller hot dogs with the same stale buns. Overcooked or rancid. Not great options.

We have chosen to review Cyber Sandwich, an EduProtocol from *The EduProtocol Field Guide, Book One,* to illustrate this point and to provide a familiar reference point as we continue to understand what makes the EduProtocols work. As you read through the description of Cyber Sandwich, think about the following questions:

- How might the activity help students learn how to think with agility?
- How might students respond to others?

- How might students work with their peers to deepen their understanding of the material presented?
- How might students use creativity in how they respond to the prompt?

If you are already familiar with Cyber Sandwich, this section will serve to refresh yourself with its elements. Don't worry, we have plenty of new protocols later in the book!

Cyber Sandwich

Students can easily copy facts from Wikipedia and create reports in minutes, but how do we move students out of the copy-and-paste cycle? By building different models that make copying and pasting irrelevant. Cyber Sandwich has three parts: students pair off and start reading independently, come back together to discuss the content and chart in a Venn diagram, then break off to write their personal responses.

Academic Goals

- To compare and contrast two like or unlike topics
- To develop skills that can be used later in larger writing projects
- To move students out of the copy+paste cycle

Teacher Big Ideas

- Create one summary paragraph that lists differences and similarities and has a conclusion.
- Start very simply and with a narrow focus.
- Expand to multiple categories as student skills grow.
- Different teams of students might focus on comparing various categories so the presentations cover a broader range of topics.

Description

In this EduProtocol, students will work in the two highest levels of Marzano's Nine Essential Instructional Strategies list from the book *Classroom Instruction That Works: Research-Based Strategies for Increasing Student Achievement*. As students record notes, compare and contrast topics, and summarize, they will begin to develop the foundational skills they can use later to digest challenging information and produce longer research reports.

Prepare for the Activity

Choose an article for the students to read. Start with one for both students. Copy the article so each student has their own or provide a digital version.

Instructions

Step 1: Students will spend ten minutes reading the article and taking notes.

Step 2: Students will spend five to ten minutes discussing their findings with their partner and completing a Venn diagram together.

Step 3: Using the shared notes and Venn diagram, each student will write their own paragraph comparing and contrasting the two topics based on the information gathered on the slides.

Step 4: Each team will take turns presenting their findings to the class, other groups, or a partner.

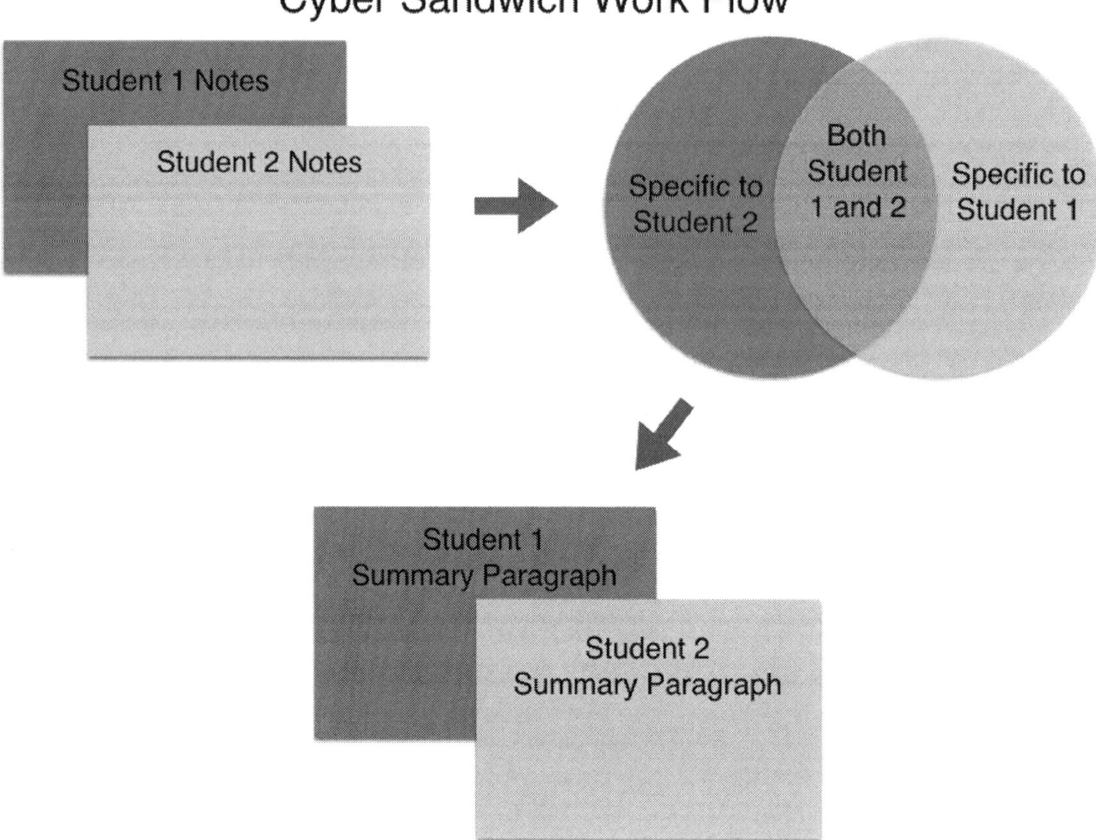

Key Points to Remember

New is messy. Proficiency builds over time. Narrow the focus, as the students are limited to writing one-paragraph summaries. It is okay to expand the categories as student proficiency increases.

Jon

Do a Cyber Sandwich on different aspects of a topic for five days, and *voila*! The research report is done! See a plan for that in Chapter 16.

Adaptation

Use articles with opposing views or topics: hamburgers vs. tacos, chocolate ice cream vs. pie, rock vs. country. Master the tech and protocol, then build up.

Adapting for Littles

An excellent starting point for littles is to use a class-wide shared story experience or short video. Also consider doing a few reps on paper to front-load students before bringing out the laptops.

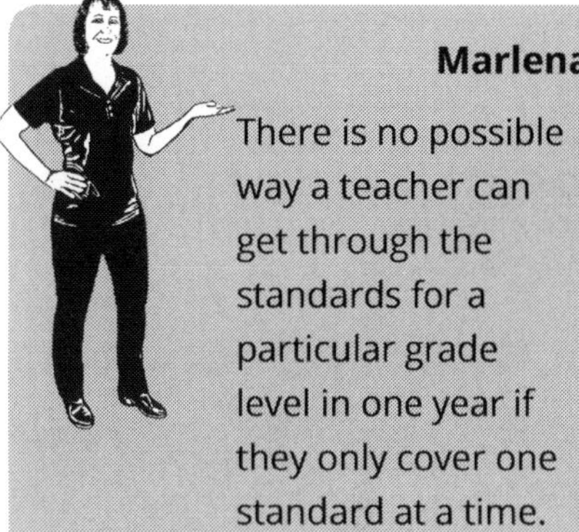

Marlena

There is no possible way a teacher can get through the standards for a particular grade level in one year if they only cover one standard at a time.

Reflect on Your Experience

Try this protocol with your students a few times and observe how they work. Think and reflect upon the experience of your students. Did you see them responding? Did you notice them using agility in their thinking and discussions? Did they work with a peer to deepen their understanding of the content? Did you observe them using creativity in how they responded to the prompt? Students are practicing many standards and skills all at once, not just one at a time. If you didn't see these things, you may need to spend some time training them in this new way of interacting.

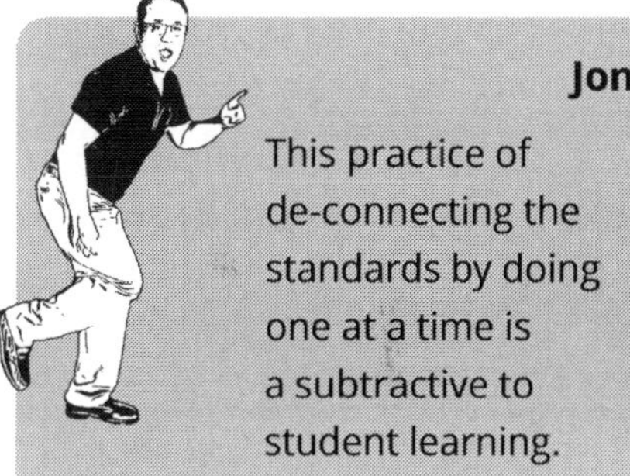

Jon

This practice of de-connecting the standards by doing one at a time is a subtractive to student learning.

Fluency with Learning Tools

What makes Cyber Sandwich a protocol? The content changes easily enough, but students will know exactly what they will be doing to tackle the curriculum when you say, "Hey kids, we are doing a Cyber Sandwich today!"

Imagine using Cyber Sandwich with an article about the relationship between the missionaries and the Indians in the settling of California, or with the signing of the Declaration of Independence, studying the conflict in *The Lord of the Flies*, the conceptual understanding of area and perimeter, or in researching another topic. What content might you use with a Cyber Sandwich in your classroom?

When you say Cyber Sandwich, students of any age will know they're going to pair off, share the document, start reading, come back together to discuss the content and put it in a Venn diagram, then break off to write their response. It is a flow they will be familiar with because you taught it to them, and now you can pull it out with a moment's notice, and everyone will know what to expect. And if they learned Cyber Sandwich last year, and you want to use it this year, they already know what to expect because their previous teacher called it a Cyber Sandwich and developed a shared vocabulary and understanding! This is how we build lesson design fluency across grades.

Now the teacher is free to roam the classroom, ask questions, answer questions about the reading, respond to individual students, or help with vocabulary. These protocols are great because they allow the teacher to provide personal feedback in real time.

Kids in this class will not be raising their hand to ask, "Teacher, what do I do now?" because they will already know what to do.

Marlena

Students using this protocol are not struggling to learn how to complete a task; instead, they are focusing on what they are learning!

Tick Tock—the Clock is Ticking

Unless they're given guidance, most students will use all available time to complete an assignment or task. Some will need even more! An essential aspect of EduProtocols is timing. The sections of activities in these EduProtocols are timed to keep students moving through the event. In *The EduProtocol Field Guide, Book One*, Jon describes living in a world of the "suck" where life comes to a standstill while we avoid the inevitable task before us. Students

Jon

Some teachers I met near Tulare, CA, call this TWA: Teaching while Walking Around (Feel free to bring your coffee!).

have little sense of time, so moving students along teaches them to finish and to feel good about finishing. Marlena's husband, Walt, always tells her that "Finished is beautiful." And indeed, this is true. Nothing is worse than a project never completed—unless it's a project never started!

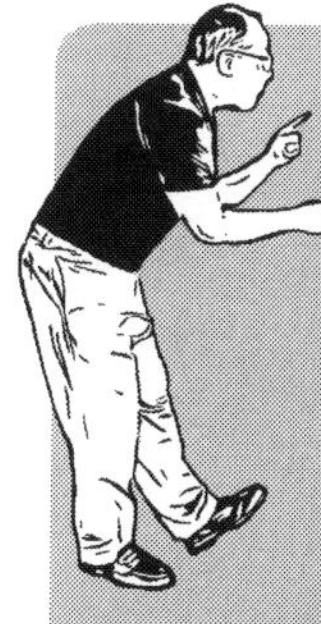

Jon

Don't go for a super-perfect first try—go for a super-fast first try. *The first rep will usually be fairly bad.* The second rep is less bad. On the third rep, magic starts happening.

As students work on learning and mastering curriculum, remember to keep them moving forward, both within a protocol and from protocol to protocol. If the protocol is taking three days, shorten it! Most of the protocols are designed so one piece of the curriculum is delivered in one period. These are chunked activities; one EduProtocol generally does not contain enough content to justify lasting two to five days, as it is not intended to be a unit in itself. Later in the book, we will address "stacking" and "smashing" to tackle longer or more complicated pieces of curriculum.

Reps

"I think this was much easier to explain in third period than it was in first period," a teacher commented to Marlena after a day of working together to refine EduProtocol implementation in a classroom. Without skipping a beat, Marlena asked, "Do you think your students might feel the same?" She could see the light bulb coming on as the teacher took a deep breath and then murmured, "I guess it would be the same for them. It should be easier tomorrow and the next day."

Jon

Reps for the win! It's always about reps.

Exactly! The first time will be rough, like playing a board game before you understand all the directions and rules. Don't worry—they'll get it on the third or fourth rep!

In the rest of this book, we will introduce twelve new EduProtocols and expand on educator-created adaptations for nine EduProtocols that were first introduced in *The EduProtocol Field Guide, Book One.*

Let the journey begin!

Call to Action

New to Protocols?

If you are new to EduProtocols, use Cyber Sandwich this week in your classroom. Be sure to implement this tool several times to give your students the benefits of repetition.

Seasoned User

We hear a lot of talk about preparing students for a future we cannot yet imagine or for jobs not yet created. While it might seem overwhelming, that task is not as far out of reach as you might believe. If you need help imagining this new world, view the YouTube film "The Last Job on Earth: Imagining a Fully Automated World" (bit.ly/lastjob) and then ask yourself, "How am I preparing my students for *this* kind of future?"

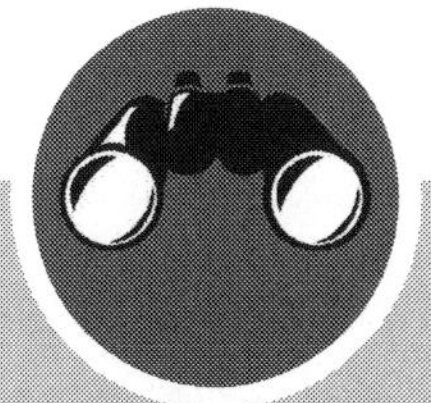

Chapter 2
A Quick *EduProtocol Field Guide*, Book One Review

I don't think I've ever wanted magic more.

—J.K. Rowling

Below is the Eight-Point PROTOCOL Checklist from *The EduProtocol Field Guide, Book One* that details the most important considerations we use when creating EduProtocols. Keep these in mind as you plan and prepare EduProtocols in your classroom or school.

Eight-Point PROTOCOL Checklist

EduProtocols are structured enough to be consistent from classroom to classroom, yet open-ended enough that students can be creative and have a choice in demonstrating their learning. The lesson design itself is relatively simple and has the ultimate goal of shifting the workload from the teacher to the student.

What makes an EduProtocol? There are eight common characteristics of EduProtocols that make them powerful tools for teaching and learning:

- **Protocol = Lesson**—If EduProtocol + EduProtocol + EduProtocol equals a unit, then one EduProtocol is somewhat equal to a lesson. They have substance and are not to be confused with "activities," which we might do within a lesson. These activities, for example, are not protocols: quick write, pair-share, gallery walk, exit tickets, elevator pitches, voting, sentence stems, writing what you learned in the form of a song, or folded-paper books for notes.

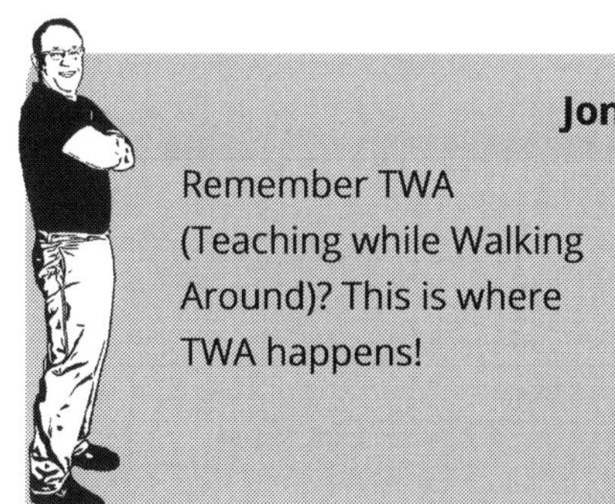

Jon
Remember TWA (Teaching while Walking Around)? This is where TWA happens!

- **Replicable**—An EduProtocol has a defined structure that can be repeated by other students and teachers. The EduProtocol should be named to provide it an identity and to separate it from the content.
- **One to One**—Accountability for each student's part in the activity is a key component of the EduProtocols. The contribution is traceable and provides evidence of learning.
- **Time Frame**—A fitness trainer wouldn't have a client do bench presses or squats for a full hour. Effective workouts have variety. EduProtocols should be ten to thirty-five minutes in length. Ideally an EduProtocol does not use the entire class period, thereby allowing students to work on multiple learning events in one period. If you need to, you can simplify the content so it can be completed in the allotted time.
- **Overtly Connected Standards**—An EduProtocol should feature multiple adopted standards (ten to twenty-five grade-level standards) in a single setting. Kids will struggle on Day 1 but will be rolling by Day 5. (See #1 and #2 under "Best Practices" below for reference.)
- **Cs in Action** (Four Cs—Communication, Collaboration, Critical Thinking, and Creativity)—Do not turn your class into an Edu-gulag with unceasing fill-in-the-blanks-type work. Effective EduProtocols are not just worksheets; they embody open-ended learning and Universal Design for Learning (UDL) concepts. If your students don't like a protocol, you are likely doing it incorrectly.
- **Open and Able to Be Used across Multiple Subject Areas**—EduProtocols should work across multiple subject areas (e.g., an EduProtocol used for science could be used with social studies and language arts) or across multiple standards within a subject (e.g., math-specific EduProtocols could be used to teach the associative property as well as factor trees).
- **Loved by Kids**—Design for children! Take your teacher hat off and tap into your own innate creativity. Design something that's irresistible to students of many ages.

Best Practices: SPIRIT

Spirit is the heart and soul of who you are, and it reflects our sincerest intent for EduProtocol implementation in your classroom. Keep SPIRIT in mind while you are deploying the EduProtocols and sharing them with your students. Below are the six big SPIRIT ideas Jon and Marlena use every day when working with kids:

Serious Commitment—We always tell our own children, "If you are going to play a sport or be in a play, commit to the whole season." You can do the same by making the commitment to use the EduProtocol weekly, all semester, or all year long so students gain fluency with the process, which will enable them to focus on the content.

Progression—The EduProtocol begins quickly and easily. The first two reps of an EduProtocol should focus on a non-academic, low-cognitive-load task so students can concentrate on the task, not the content. Educators should simply focus on helping students complete the EduProtocols. Quality may be low at first. Over time you can add skills and subtasks or shorten the time frame to add intensity.

Immediate Feedback—If you are grading an EduProtocol any time other than immediately, your EduProtocol is in danger of losing student intensity. Athletes crave feedback. Chefs come out of the kitchen to see how guests enjoyed the meal. Develop for immediate feedback, and you'll see a more immediate impact.

Reps—Jon's football coach, Mike Waufle, loved to say, "Reactions are what you do without thinking. The only way to get the very best results is to do a million reps." We can't do a million reps in class, but we can do twenty or thirty (or more), and that's mastery-level learning.

Interest—Keep the pace just fast enough to hold the attention of kids by giving them the right amount of content for the right amount of time.

Tech Balance—Please use tools like Quizizz, Kahoot, Google Suite, Flipgrid, and others, but remember: Sometimes paper is faster. Brain research tells us a good, old Frayer or Venn diagram on paper can be a super-efficient way to set up for the digital tools that help ideas get synthesized.

EduProtocols are fairly simple to deploy. The PROTOCOL and SPIRIT checklists provide an important framework for the implementation of new EduProtocols in our quest to deepen student engagement, creativity, and outcomes.

Go Slow to Go Fast

Great teachers take time in the first weeks of school to update students on classroom procedures: where to get the paper, when to sharpen pencils, how to put away the laptops, and how to exit the classroom. Jon's and Marlena's classrooms ran smoothly because they each took the time to make sure their kids knew how to move in both the physical and virtual classroom spaces.

We positioned our classrooms so as to not micromanage students. In our respective classrooms, we needed to be able to sit with a group of students or lean into a child's math work while the rest of the room ran itself in an orderly manner. Experienced teachers understand the importance of training students in the first days of school, yet when it comes to lesson design, it is easy to forget that we also need to train students in how to learn in the virtual environment! The EduProtocols will provide a structure to help you set expectations for your class.

A common mistake made when teachers begin to deploy EduProtocols in their lessons is to start out too fast with *too much* content. Learning the protocol is hard enough without also having to learn new content at the same time! We will explain why in greater detail later. For now, just remember to start slowly in terms of content. Teach just the protocol and use light or fun content that students are already familiar with, such as Disney characters, pop culture, or school rules. Once kids get the protocol part down, you can speed up and deliver all kinds of complicated content. Your students will know what to do and how to do it, allowing them—and you—to focus on the content!

Marlena

I've made the mistake of jumping into content too fast several times. I have regretted it every time. It seems kids either get confused, or we don't finish on time.

Templates

We have provided several templates on our website, eduprotocols.com, to help you get started. These templates will structure the EduProtocol for students and simplify the deployment process and learning curve. As you and your students become more adept at using the EduProtocols, consider minimizing the structure you provide and allowing students a more open and free canvas in which to design. You'll see their creativity shine as they learn to use the space given to them!

Call to Action

New to Protocols?

If EduProtocols are new for you, reread the directions for Cyber Sandwich in the previous chapter and reflect upon how the PROTOCOL checklist is exemplified through Cyber Sandwich. Then use Cyber Sandwich with students and think about how SPIRIT reinforces best practices with the deployment of the protocol.

Seasoned User

If you have read *The EduProtocol Field Guide, Book One* and are already using EduProtocols, think about the last EduProtocol you used with your students. With that in mind, reflect upon the SPIRIT checklist and think about areas that might be improved upon in your deployment of EduProtocols. Implement one or more of these strategies immediately.

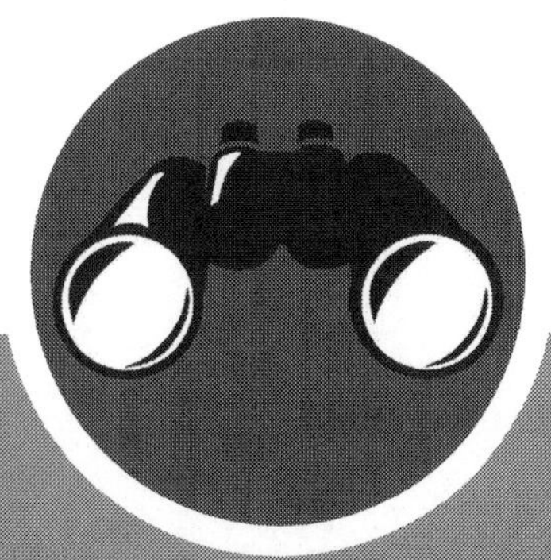

SECTION 2
A Guide to New EduProtocols

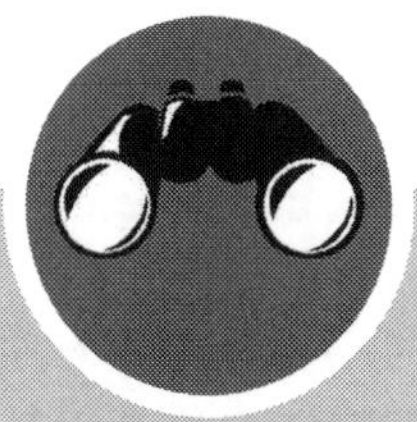

Chapter 3
Sketch and Tell EduProtocol

Read this (super-long, boring) essay/article/selection from the book, post your reflection to the forum, and comment on the posts of three other peers.

Do you remember seeing this kind of assignment in online or college courses? Marlena and her high school media teacher/instructional design husband, Walt, created Sketch and Tell as an alternative to this standby activity. Use Sketch and Tell to facilitate visual representation, discussion, and explanatory writing across grade levels!

Description

Students create a visual image (similar to a digital sketch note) of the central concept. They pair-share and explain their image to a partner, then individually write an explanatory paragraph.

Academic Goals

- To link multiple forms of representation within one assignment
- To develop a conceptual understanding of content
- To support explanatory writing

Teacher Big Ideas

- Pair-share precedes writing to support conceptual understanding.
- Think through the creation of an original explanatory image or diagram.
- Require students to draw original images or use simple line drawings.

Prepare for the Activity

Step 1: (optional) Prepare a template for the activity to share with students.

Step 2: Link a reading passage, textbook selection, or video to the assignment.

Instructions

Step 1: Students will work in pairs on this assignment. Share assignment with pairs of students or allow them to share with a partner.

Step 2: Students read or watch the attached video material and then create a digital sketch depicting the main idea(s).

Step 3: Students explain their digital sketches to a partner or a small group.

Step 4: Students write an explanatory paragraph summarizing the central concept of the material.

Sketch and	Tell
After reading or watching a video, sketch your diagram, chart, or image here.	After sharing your sketch, write about it here.

Key Points to Remember

- This assignment is about making an *original* image and explaining the meaning of one's work.
- Time each of the three parts of the assignment to keep kids moving at a pace that encourages engagement.
- Maintain a fun energy level (e.g., play music while they're working).

Modification

Use a jigsaw format such as the Iron Chef EduProtocol found in *The EduProtocol Field Guide, Book One* so the class can collectively cover a broader range of material. Allow students to present their infographic to the class in short presentations.

English Language Learner Tip: *Encourage ELLs to use academic language when talking with partners by using sentence frames and modeling. Try using a handout with a key word or phrase for students to reference during pair-shares.*

Adapting for Littles

- Littles will need help learning how to use the drawing features of their platform. Start by providing some elements of the image (lines and pre-colored shapes) to get kids started faster.
- Keep the activity open-ended for littles so they can practice choice in their work.
- Start with class projects and work to the individual level.
- Have littles take notes before going to the computer but keep them basic and simple. Littles tend to put all their effort into paper-and-pencil and are then finished by the time computers are brought out. Avoid having littles copy paperwork to the computer—this is a waste of their time.

Consider learning this EduProtocol on paper and then transitioning to the computer once students understand the flow of the activity.

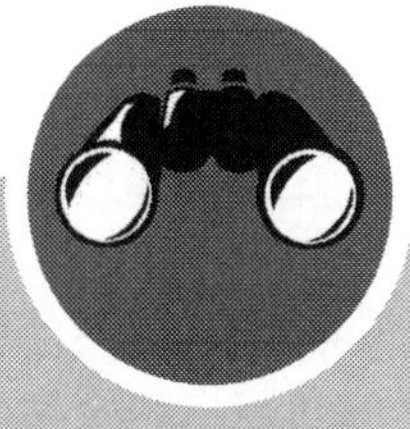

Chapter 4
Thin Slide EduProtocol

Contributed by Steven J. McGriff, PhD (@stevemcgriff)

There is quite a history to the thin-slide/thick-slide story. Jon has forever used the thick slide as a report format. A "report" slide is basically a deconstructed paragraph—title, subtitle, five to six facts, two to three pictures, and a couple of citations. They are a *super* way to scaffold report writing, but they're not a great way to "present." The other kind of slide is very lean—one word and one picture, based on the Lawrence Lessig design constraint. Realizing the aesthetics of the two slides are polar opposites, Jon started calling them Thin and Thick slides. Following Jon's Thin and Thick slide designations, Steven McGriff adapted the Thin Slide EduProtocol. Sometimes we need a full, thick slide for depth (again, all the makings of a full paragraph), but sometimes one slide and one word will get the job done, and that's where the thin slide can be helpful. It is an entry-level, "low-floor, high-ceiling" type of activity that can be used for developing students' language, vocabulary, content knowledge, visual literacy, and creative expression through a simple, minimalist-style slide design. Instead of taking a long time to make a so-so slide deck, the Thin Slide EduProtocol helps students make a great slide deck quickly!

Description

Each student creates a *single* slide to be part of a larger class slide deck. Each student slide contains *one* word and *one* image (no more, as speed is the goal). The teacher gives a key concept, such as a word, concept, or theme, for students to explore in five minutes, and they are to build one slide in that timeframe using their choice of a word and image that relates to the prompt. After creating a Thin Slide, students give an eight- to twelve-second presentation from their seats and describe their slide in a whip-around fashion. Quickly getting input from the entire class is the main goal of Thin Slides.

Academic Goals

- To achieve quick academic concept development (Imagine thirty-five slides about a single vocab word or concept made in five minutes and presented in another six to seven minutes.)
- To create less work for the teacher and way more contact time with the content for students
- To focus on creativity and visual communication
- To support students' collaboration and critical thinking
- To address the CCSS ELA literacy standards for speaking and listening, writing, and language

Teacher Big Ideas

- Limit the need for direct instruction.
- Use Thin Slides as a pre- or post-instruction activity.
- Why so fast? We want 100 percent participation. Limiting the time allows more students to be engaged.
- Build student skills and speed to prepare them for using other protocols (Iron Chef, BookaKucha, and Cyber Sandwich) with a bare minimum of prep.

Prepare for the Activity

- Determine the key term or concept for the activity; for example, similar angles, a shape name, a vocab word (a Latin root or a CVVC word), an abstract noun, a civic-minded word like "freedom," or a reflection of a unit of study.
- Make a shareable slide deck with the term or details on Slide 1 and any other details you'd like to add. Share with students. (Optional: make a single blank slide for as many students as you have.)

Note: *Remember to do two to three fun practice runs with a low academic load to practice. It only takes ten to fifteen minutes to play a round during Smart Start. The sharing is done in a whip-around format.*

Marlena

Remember that as kids develop speed and fluency with one slide, show them some of the elements of design such as image on the thirds, how to choose complementary colors on the color wheel, or other tips.

If you could change one thing in the world, what would it be?

Instructions

Step 1: Model the format of having one word and one image on a slide to help students understand what they are to produce.

Share the class slide deck and the prompt with your class.

Number students so they know on which slide to begin working.

Step 2: Set a four-minute timer for students to explore the prompt and create a slide with one word and one image.

Step 3: Students share about their slide in a whip-around manner: eight seconds maximum per student. The whole activity will be made up of the soundbites each student contributes.

Key Points to Remember

- This is a fast activity—use a timer and enforce the time.
- This is a *simple* activity—the power is in thirty-five shares, not in thirty-five perfect slides.

- This activity could lead to a discussion or follow a discussion.
- This is useful for review of a unit or topic of study, as each student contributes one key idea.
- Topics are endless for Thin Slides both in terms of content and creative expression with visuals: presidents, key math terms, literary devices, science terms/concepts, grammar errors, spelling errors, abstract nouns, reflections, anything that can be expressed in visual terms. (Isn't that everything?)

Adapting for Littles

Thin slides are pretty simple, but to help the littles, have them use the "Explore" button in Google Slides, or try using a pre-selected folder of images for students to choose from so no searching is needed. Make sure to have at least twenty pics so they don't overuse one image (create complexity by adding a few non-example images to the options). Create a Thin Slide deck based on a vocabulary word set, putting one word on a different slide and ask students to find an appropriate picture for their assigned slide. Try allowing students to work in pairs to support one another.

Presentation Tip: *If using Google Classroom or another similar learning management system, assign individual slides to students. To mimic a single slide deck, open student work in the grading window, where flipping from one slide to the next is easy.*

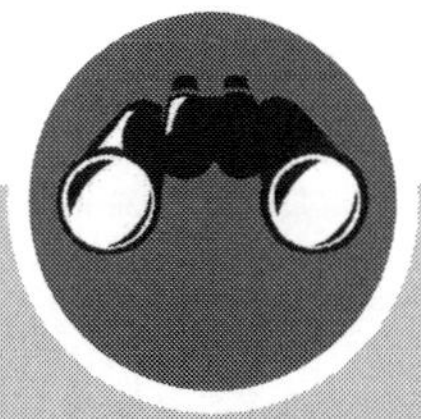

Chapter 5
Speed Geeking EduProtocol: Math Chats

Created by Daniel Kaufmann (@KauDan721)

There are quite a few educators who have developed strategies and activities for the classroom that follow a "speed dating" format. Daniel Kaufmann, math teacher and instructional coach, has reimagined this strategy for the math classroom with an emphasis on the chat!

Description

Students create one slide about their topic and then explain their slide to a partner. In the fashion of speed dating, students move to another partner and repeat the explanation. They then move to a third partner and repeat again, refining the explanation a little more each time.

Academic Goals

- To develop succinct explanations for math concepts
- To increase understanding of material learned
- To develop academic language

Teacher Big Ideas

- The answer is not the goal.
- Repetition develops fluency and mastery.
- Grow experts through peer-to-peer teaching.

Prepare for the Activity

Create a blank slide deck with one slide per student.

Instructions

Day 1: Introduce the problem on which students will be working.

Discuss strategies for working and solving the problem.

Day 2: Introduce a similar problem using different numbers.

Discuss strategies for working and solving the problem.

Day 3: Introduce a third similar problem using different numbers.

Discuss strategies for working and solving the problem.

Day 4: Provide a collection of problems similar to the problem introduced on Day 1.

Students choose one problem, then they find and explain their strategy for solving that problem. Students may add additional slides to explain different approaches to the same problem.

Each student shares one strategy with another student.

Students find a second partner and repeat the strategy using the same problem as the first rotation.

Students find a third partner and repeat the strategy using the same problem as the first rotation.

Note: *Sharing has two parts for each partner. Partner A should share first, followed by Partner B.*

Key Points to Remember

- The answer is not the focus; really good strategies are.
- Students should work to perfect their explanation by the third round.
- Reps for the win!

Adapting for Littles

This activity is easily adapted for littles, as they are building just one slide, and the majority of the activity on Day 4 centers on talking about the strategies used. Try practicing using paper before involving technology, as technology adds complexity. Consider creating "pre-built" images and numbers on the sides of the slide as a template. Students can add these to their slide as needed.

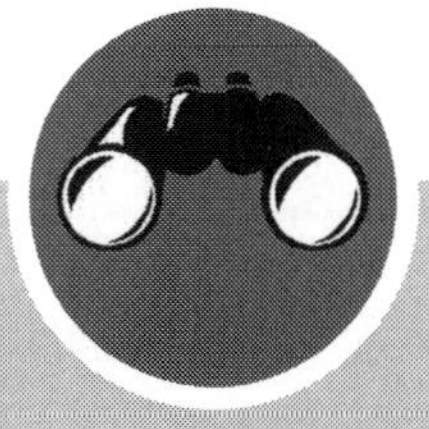

Chapter 6
Speed Geeking EduProtocol: Persuasive Arguments

Created by Daniel Kaufmann (@KauDan721)

Students use the power of repetition to refine their position for or against a topic in this Speed Geeking EduProtocol developed by Daniel Kaufmann, math teacher and instructional coach.

Description

Students have a limited amount of time to take a position, create an argument, and complete several repetitions to practice and refine their pitch.

Academic Goals

To enable students to . . .

- Make a pitch
- Listen and respond to peers
- Prepare for writing persuasive arguments

Teacher Big Ideas

- Get kids talking
- Practice makes better
- Verbal articulation supports writing

Prepare for the Activity

Choose a variety of grade-level-appropriate prompts for students to use for practice

- Create a slide deck for introducing the prompts to students.
- Create a blank slide deck for student responses on Days 2, 3, and 4.

Instructions

Day 1: Introduce the EduProtocol and show students one sample prompt.

Discuss possible viewpoints for and against along with thoughts, wonderings, and ideas related to the prompt. Keep Day 1 verbal.

Day 2: Show students a new but similar subject matter sample prompt.

Students create a slide for the class-wide shared deck detailing their thoughts, wonderings, and/or ideas related to the prompt. Once the slides are completed, discuss possible viewpoints for and against along with thoughts, wonderings, and ideas related to the prompt.

Tip: *Students should be given about five minutes to create their slide with a few notes. Treat this as a quick write in which the goal is to develop agility of thinking.*

Day 3: Show students a new but similar subject matter sample prompt.

Repeat the procedure for Day 2.

Day 4:

Step 1: Allow students to choose a prompt from a list you have provided. These may be similar in topic, theme, or difficulty.

Step 2: Students spend ten minutes planning to present possible viewpoints for or against the topic.

Step 3: Students share their thoughts with a partner.

(Optional: Allow for one minute of timed feedback to the presenter per cycle.)

Step 4: Students choose a new partner and share again.

Step 5: Students choose a third partner and share again. By this third time, the student should have a fairly refined "pitch" of their viewpoint.

Key Points to Remember

- The value is in the sharing.
- Model topics related or similar to those you've planned for Day 4.
- Be sure the students understand what is expected on Day 4 and model that behavior on Days 1, 2, and 3.

Variation: *On Days 1, 2, and 3 (and possibly even on Day 4), roll a die to decide if the class is discussing the* for *or* against *argument. Be sure to mix and match topics with points of view to develop adeptness in students. The goal is that students, with practice, will be able to effectively speak to multiple points of view.*

Adapting for Littles

It is never too early to begin developing the verbal and thinking skills students will need to effectively defend or debate a point! Littles can successfully participate in this protocol when the process is simplified. Choose simple topics that littles can relate to, and then model on Days 1 and 2. On Day 3 students will replicate the process with a new topic you have chosen for them or for the class. Be sure to model exactly what the students will be expected to do. Facilitate pair-share, and then ask some students to share with the class. On Day 4 students create one slide with their "argument." Extend the creation experience by allowing students to share key points from their slide.

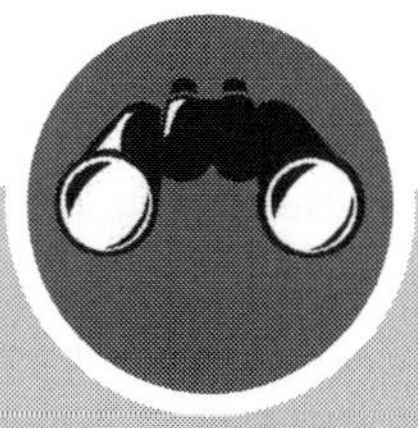

Chapter 7
The Ultimate Exit Ticket EduProtocol

Created by Jeremiah Ruesch (@mathkaveli)

Jeremiah, a math teacher, developed this protocol adaptation of the classic exit ticket for his math class as he was looking for ways to help students reflect upon and develop mathematical concepts over a period of time. The Ultimate Exit Ticket evolved into a more authentic way to track growth with his students.

Description

Students reflect daily on the concepts they have learned. The five-slide sequence is added to each day and completed by the fifth day to present to peers or the class. (Note: The space at the bottom of the slides for the speaker notes makes a useful space for writing! When students present their slides, the written notes are automatically hidden, leaving only the illustration for viewing.)

Academic Goals

- To solidify conceptual understanding of complex ideas
- To promote growth over time
- To allow for reflection on progress

Teacher Big Ideas

- Students are building on their work over the five days.
- Exit tickets provide a snapshot into a student's understanding.
- Correcting prior work may not be possible until students understand the concept.
- Use multiple modes of illustrating, writing, speaking, and reflection.

Prepare for the Activity

Prepare five slides for students in a template or allow students to create their own.

Instructions

Day 1: At the end of the period, students take a few minutes to create a slide that represents what they have learned that day. They will use the drawing features of their chosen platform to illustrate the concepts and then write about what they learned. The writing could be either a reflection or an explanation. Structure this part according to curricular goals.

Day 2: Repeat.

Day 3: Repeat.

Day 4: Repeat.

Day 5: Repeat and pair-share one or more of the slides with a partner or present to the class in the style of Pecha Kucha (one slide every twenty seconds) or Thin Slides (6–10 second share-out for one slide per student.)

***Note:** Consider pair-sharing on the fifth day instead of building the fifth side.*

Modification

This activity lets students present in different ways. You can try calling on random students to present one or more slides and asking the group to choose the best slide from each student or allowing students to browse and comment on the work of their peers.

Key Points to Remember

- Use for a sneak peek into how students understand the content.
- Use daily in order to build skills not only on the computer but also in illustrating mathematical and other concepts.

- Students are building the slides as they learn. They may need to go back and correct errors from the beginning of the sequence.

Adapting for Littles

- Littles will need more time, so keep the concepts simple for this one-a-day activity. Start small and build up to increase both skill level and speed.
- Try adding to a slide deck every few days instead of daily.
- Consider making a class book showing the concepts they have learned. More students can participate in a class book if they are assigned to groups of four.

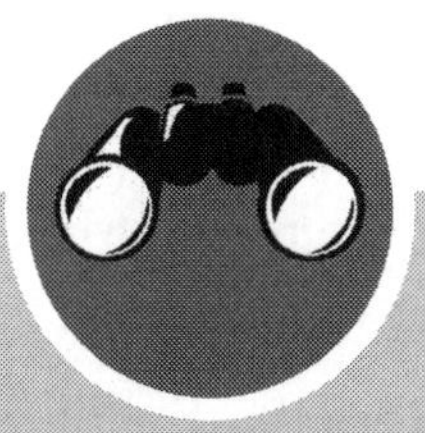

Chapter 8
Emoji Power Paragraph EduProtocol

The Random Emoji Generator was created by Ian Byrd as a fun tool for students to use. Ian also makes a series of videos for gifted students available at byrdseed.tv. Jon happened upon the Random Emoji Generator one day and created this protocol around its use. He developed it as a writing prompt inspired by Robert C. Pinckert's book *Pinckert's Practical Grammar*. What inspired Jon most was Pinckert's explanation of writing a paragraph as pursuing an idea, not the listing of elements or events. Pinckert redefined how Jon taught paragraph writing and moved him away from the standard hamburger formula.

Description

As a former K–8 and high school level classroom teacher, I was always disappointed to see kids who were being trained that a paragraph should follow this format of *I am going to tell you . . . and then firstly, secondly, thirdly. In closing, thanks for reading my paragraph.* This isn't what an authentic paragraph looks or sounds like. It's a nice brief stage for training, but it seems that all too often that's where educators stall out in their modeling.

I am quite a fan of Robert Pinckert and his book *Pinckert's Practical Grammar*. I love his approach to how a paragraph should be formed. Pinckert says that the essence of a paragraph is to *pursue an idea*. That's the single focus on how I teach paragraphing.

What if there were a faster, more organic way to teach paragraphs? A method that has scaffolds, but allows a less strict approach and ignites student imaginations?

Enter the Random Emoji Power Paragraph! I love using edtech, and I'm a huge fan of kids doing more of the thinking and not using worksheets in my classroom. (I hope you like my essay so far.)

I recently had an epiphany that led to a mashup of pedagogy and edtech that can make this teaching-of-paragraphs task exponentially more interesting, engaging, and easier for teachers to lead.

By using Ian Byrd's super-fun Random Emoji Generator website and Socrative Short answer quizzes together, I've seen a surge in paragraph writing skills. The combination of five randomly generated emoji and immediate feedback via Socrative is pure magic.

How does the Random Emoji Power Paragraph Eduprotocol work? It's super easy. That's the best part. Google, Random Emoji Generator. The site is made by an educator (Thanks, Ian Byrd!) and doesn't have any of the not-ready-for-school emoji.

Then start up a Socrative Short Answer Quiz. Once the students are logged in, the fun begins. Socrative Short Answer quizzes literally take 5–10 seconds to set up. I do Socrative Short Answer quizzes for all kinds of one sentence, open-ended assignments. By doing this four to five times a day with immediate feedback, I have moved this from an assignment to an Eduprotocol. (Find more free Eduprotocol templates at Eduprotocols.com.)

Academic Goals

- To pursue a singular idea in a paragraph
- To build fluidity in students' ability to think and respond
- To practice and develop writing skills

Teacher Big Ideas

- Scaffolding is built right in.
- For our advanced students, it challenges them to create within defined parameters.
- For ELLs and SPED (special education) students, it provides just enough scaffolding for success.

- Have fun with this one—it might get a little silly, and that is ok!

Prepare for the Activity

Step 1: Be prepared to project the Random Emoji Generator to the whole class.

Create an open-ended question in a quiz program such as Socrative. (Socrative allows for a voting feature that we will use in a bit!)

Instructions

Step 1: Explain the concept of pursuing an idea. Staying on topic is what defines a paragraph. If you pursue a new idea, it's time for a new paragraph. And for this activity, we are only writing one paragraph.

Click the Start Over button on the Random Emoji page until the class yells "yes" to pick the first emoji. This begins the game. Give the students about a minute or two to get the first sentence typed out.

Launch a one-question, short-answer quiz in Socrative.

Students write a sentence based on the emoji in the Socrative answer field of their question.

Step 2: Then hit the And Then button. Another random emoji appears. We repeat this until each student has five sentences typed. When they have five sentences, they hit submit.

When everyone is done, I select Start Vote in Socrative, and the students and I can read everyone's paragraph. It's great for them to immediately admire one another's work. And I can give pointers immediately, because we will usually do one more paragraph right away. The Start Vote option in socrative is magical, because all the students see all the work immediately—no "collecting" or handing in.

Step 3: The Random Emoji Power Paragraph can have endless permutations, making it effective for most any grade level. Once kids can snap off five to six sentences on point

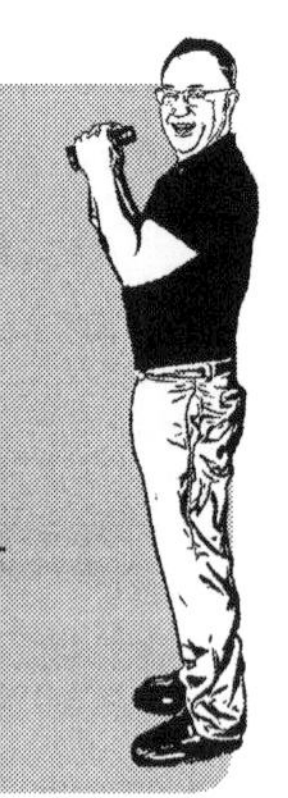

Jon

To up the difficulty, randomly throw in sentence types: a prepositional phrase, compare and contrast, or an exclamation!

(should take about six to eight reps), I will add twists like tense, point of view, literary devices, appositives and so on. I can scaffold their writing in a myriad of ways and the combination of random emoji and fast feedback via Socrative is a total win for kids and teachers.

Variations (Jon calls them "upgrades" in this protocol):

Upgrade 1: Students write the first sentence with their table peers and present their idea to the class. The class votes on one and then everyone uses that sentence as their first sentence. This step helps them pursue the same idea—although they will surely deviate by the end of five sentences!

Upgrade 2: If your class is working on 8 pARTS and Sentence pARTS from *The EduProtocol Field Guide, Book One*, then require them to use words or elements learned from those EduProtocols in some of their sentences; for example, you can incorporate learning about the structure of sentence parts by requiring that the next sentence be a compound sentence or use an appositive or an injunction. We call this "layering on the standards" to provide additional practice in writing.

Upgrade 3: Randomly choose the sentence type from Sentence Parts!

Upgrade 4: Random Emoji Power Paragraph Side Dish: Nacho Paragraph

What do you call a paragraph that's not yours? Well, it's "Nacho Paragraph"!

When teachers are using the Random Emoji Power Paragraph, there are a lot of paragraphs flying around in class. A lot. A really interesting way to maximize student growth is immediate feedback, but that can mean a lot of reading for teachers.

Here's how to get even more out of each paragraph students write in a Random Emoji Power Paragraph lesson:

Once students have completed a round of REPP, have them copy/paste some else's paragraph into a Google Doc and do one change: change the POV, change the tense, add an appositive or complex sentence, or just peer edit. Then students can resubmit in Socrative or a Google Form and see what other students did with their work.

This is a super-fast way to get this kind of feedback, and increase student growth!

Key Points to Remember

- This is a training tool, so use it until students are adroit at navigating flexible paragraph writing.
- Use in spurts to build adeptness in students.
- Scaffold with standards to give depth and rigor to writing practice.

Adapting for Littles

Littles are loving this protocol! Shorten the number of sentences to fit their growing ability and add more as students become fluent in writing. When writing just one or two sentences, consider using the question feature in Google Classroom. This feature allows them to see their peers' writing. Instead of voting, just share or allow time to read some of their peers' work. If your students are not writing independently yet, structure this protocol as a class-wide shared writing activity.

For pre- and early writers, use the Random Emoji Generator in a verbal-only format to give them practice pursuing a singular idea.

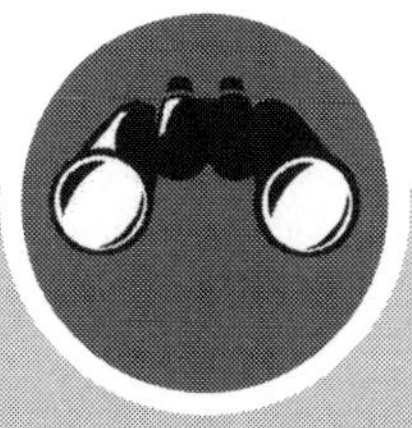

Chapter 9
Research EduProtocol

Created by Brigheen Houghton

Have you ever asked students to research a topic for a paper and found that a few were ill-equipped to do so, especially our high-risk students such as English-language learners, low readers, and special education students? Look closely at their entire body of work, including the research they are using to write their paper. Is it organized? Are the citations correct? Are there enough sources? If students have not curated adequate research resources going into the writing stage, they are behind before they even start! In this protocol, developed by master librarian and English teacher Brigheen Houghton, students will put their heads together to find, curate, and prepare the research needed for writing a research paper.

Description

Students with the same topic conduct collaborative research and then use the shared research to write individual essays or reports.

Academic Goals

- To develop context vocabulary
- To develop basic understanding of the concept to be researched
- To structure the text
- To cite evidence properly

Teacher Big Ideas

- Scaffold for weaker students by allowing them to utilize the research of peers so they begin the report-writing phase with the same resources as stronger students.

- Organize research for writing.

Prepare for the Activity

Step 1: Develop an essential open-ended question the students will use to guide their research.

Step 2: Provide an article or video students will read or watch to build shared background knowledge of the topic.

Step 3: Create a spreadsheet for fact finding. Students will place their findings on the spreadsheet.

Note: *Facts may be added in various forms such as phrases, sentences, or quotations.*

Website Source	*Facts*	*Citation*
mountvernon.org/ george-washington/ biography/	*George wanted to join the British Navy, but his mother would not let him.*	*mountvernon.org* *Mount Vernon Ladies' Association, George Washington, Accessed 12.8.2018*

Instructions

Step 1: Present students with the essential question and the article or media to view. (If reading an article, consider incorporating close reading or other annotation methods you are already using with your students.)

Step 2: Students will search for supporting information to answer the essential question and will add their findings to the shared spreadsheet. Citations should include the title of the article, title of the webpage, web address, and date accessed. Since we are crowdsourcing the research, it should take considerably less time than if done individually. Typically this phase takes about twenty to thirty minutes to complete.

Step 3: As a class, in groups, or individually, depending on the age and ability of students, review the articles for authenticity and their ability to respond to the essential question.

***Note:** This is the time to help students filter out and discuss "fake news" and the reasons why some sources are more reliable than others.*

Step 4: Students write their summary, report, or essay using the research from the shared spreadsheet.

***English Language Learner Tip:** Increasing classroom interactions for ELLs will help students find their place in the classroom and connect to their peers.*

Slide Deck Variation:

In groups of two to four students, conduct research and collect notes on a slide deck using one resource per slide. Citations should contain relevant notes, images, and quotes. Citations for sources may be added to the notes section of the slide.

At the end of the research phase, students will present their findings to their teammates.

Allow time for the teams to explore the research findings of their group and identify the three to four best sources. All team members should be familiar with these sources.

Optional: Students may copy the shared slide deck and then order it according to the sources that will be most useful to them.

Students then use the shared resources to write *independently.*

Key Points to Remember

- Discuss key searching terms appropriate for the project.
- Review credible and non-credible resources.
- Structure with scaffolding to allow success for all students.

Adapting for Littles

- Littles can use a single book, text, or website for their research. Try creating a mini-website for students to access. Structure the website like a real website, just big enough to contain the needed information and a few images to spark curiosity. One to two pages with emerging text, images, and video is just enough to support beginning website navigation skills for early and non-readers.

- Read through the sources provided with the students prior to the activity.
- Allow the class to curate information together in one classroom slide deck, with each student contributing one fact.
- Be sure to gather the children around and review all the facts they've discovered.
- Spread the project over three to four days, with just enough time (fifteen to twenty minutes) to work on one section of the project at a time.

  Day 1: Pre-read the "research"
  Day 2: Conduct research
  Day 3: Write
  Day 4: Share

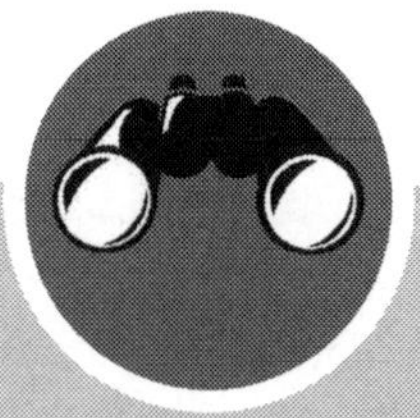

Chapter 10
Number Mania EduProtocol

Daryl was almost giddy as he began digging into the facts about the Civil War for his infographic. When he found something interesting, he would shout across the room to his teacher.

"Hey, did you know that there were 625,000 soldiers killed in the Civil War?"

"Look here. History.com says that two percent of the population died, and that is the equivalent of six million men today."

"Hey, four hundred women disguised themselves as men so they could fight!"

"Wait, wait. White soldiers were paid $13 a month, and black soldiers were paid $10 a month? Why weren't they paid the same?"

The class was reading the book *Behind Rebel Lines: The Incredible Story of Emma Edmonds, Civil War Spy* by Seymour Reit and were creating infographics to explore the book's connections to WWII.

"Do you like history?" I asked, midway into the period.

"Noooo, I like math," Daryl answered.

During cleanup Daryl rose out of his chair and, mid-step to the Chromebook cart, turned and announced to no one in particular, "Man, I can't believe I finished a project for once!"

Infographics are number-oriented, visual representations of data or research results and are perfect for engaging kids who view numbers as a way of understanding the world. Daryl's teacher was also surprised that Daryl, a continuation high school student, finished a project for once! She commented after class, "It was good to see Daryl taking an interest in something for a change."

Jon

This activity is AWESOME for developing symbology and metaphorical imagery for students by DISALLOWING a Google Image Search. It's magical in its simplicity and academic demands.

Description

Students work at a deeper level of comprehension to create an original infographic (number and fact-based poster) depicting information and content covered. Students then comment and reflect on the work of peers. Students create their infographic using only the shapes and lines within the slide or PowerPoint program or icons from The Noun Project, a collection of simplified images. Otherwise they may not use premade images or photos since this is a poster about facts, numbers, and statistics. The focus should be on representation and communication of those facts in the most straightforward manner possible, pushing students not only to visualize the big ideas of the content but also to construct those ideas based on their understanding of it.

Academic Goals

- To construct a visual and oral understanding of content
- To reflect and comment thoughtfully on the work of peers
- To summarize findings

Teacher Big Ideas

- Infographics convey numbers and data in a visual format to increase comprehension.
- Students learn to comment constructively on the work of peers.
- Students internalize the content as they analyze data and put it in a visual format.

Prepare for the Activity

Step 1: Choose the topic of study.

Step 2: Find samples of infographics to share with students. (Search Google Images for student-made infographics.)

Step 3: Prepare a shared spreadsheet for the crowdsourced collection of data and facts. Note: Spreadsheets work well for the data collection process.

Number Mania Data Collection Form			
Number	Fact	Source	Name

Step 4: Create a customized slide or drawing that is 8"x14", 14"x8", or a similarly long and skinny size that is typical of many infographics.

Step 5: (Optional) Place a collection of infographic icons from The Noun Project along the sides of the slide for students to use.

Marlena

Crowdsourcing the data collection process in your classroom speeds up the research time and allows students to use a broader range of data points than they can find on their own.

Instructions

Step 1: Introduce infographics to students by showing them several sample images and talking about the elements on the infographic. (Number-centric with short, impactful data points.)

Step 2: Students conduct research from the printed reading material, teacher-curated websites, or the internet to gather facts for their infographic and paste their facts into a class-wide shared spreadsheet. Be sure students include the link to the original source in the spreadsheet or in bibliographic information later so other students can verify the number.

English Language Learner Tip: *Classroom sourced research is one activity that engages English Language Learners with the culture of the classroom. Regardless of their ability, all students can contribute to the classroom-shared spreadsheet. Boost opportunities to provide meaningful contributions by providing options for leveled reading materials.*

Collected Data for the American Civil War			
Number	**Fact**	**Source**	**Name**
1863	Emancipation Proclamation	https://www.battlefields.org/learn/articles/10-facts-what-everyone-should-know-about-civil-war?gclid=Cj0KCQiAoJrfBRC0ARIsANqkS_5sapNz3-G5zutEac3_cpC_e4URQOwkDssNcYWGnklTRkimBoNwELEaAoMbEALw_wcB	Daryl
4 million	Number of slaves in the south	https://en.wikipedia.org/wiki/American_Civil_War	Katelyn
52,000	Battle near Gettysburg, Pennsylvania	https://www.battlefields.org/learn/articles/10-facts-what-everyone-should-know-about-civil-war?gclid=Cj0KCQiAoJrfBRC0ARIsANqkS_5sapNz3-G5zutEac3_cpC_e4URQOwkDssNcYWGnklTRkimBoNwELEaAoMbEALw_wcB	Melissa
4	Length of the Civil War in years (1861-1865)	https://www.battlefields.org/learn/articles/10-facts-what-everyone-should-know-about-civil-war?gclid=Cj0KCQiAoJrfBRC0ARIsANqkS_5sapNz3-G5zutEac3_cpC_e4URQOwkDssNcYWGnklTRkimBoNwELEaAoMbEALw_wcB	Jonathan
620,000	Men who died	https://www.battlefields.org/learn/articles/10-facts-what-everyone-should-know-about-civil-war?gclid=Cj0KCQiAoJrfBRC0ARIsANqkS_5sapNz3-G5zutEac3_cpC_e4URQOwkDssNcYWGnklTRkimBoNwELEaAoMbEALw_wcB	Rayne
23	Union States	https://www.history.com/topics/american-civil-war/american-civil-war-history	Sandy
11	Confederate States	https://www.history.com/topics/american-civil-war/american-civil-war-history	Rick

Step 3: Show students how the elements in their drawing program (Google Drawing or Google Slides, for example) can be used to create an infographic. Discuss design elements such as lines, shapes, simple images, titles, and numbers.

Step 4: Students create their infographic, using numbers and facts from the crowdsourced document for the data.

Step 5: Students share their infographic with peers.

Step 6: Students comment on the infographics of at least three to four other students. Provide guidelines for constructive comments appropriate for these peer reviews. There are many samples and models for peer-to-peer feedback, but one easy way to start is to have students provide comments in two categories: positive comments and question comments.

Positive comments:

What impressed me was . . .

You helped me understand . . .

It had a big impact on me when . . .

Question comments:

Why do . . . ?

Have you considered . . . ?

What are . . . ?

Step 7: (Optional) Students revise their infographics based on feedback from peers.

Jon

The Noun Project is a great place to find simple images for inserting into student work. Go to thenounproject.com or install the Noun Project Google Add-On for use within Google Slides at bit.ly/The-Noun-Project

Key Points to Remember

- Start small.
- Keep it moving.
- Maintain simplicity all around (data and images).

California Gold Rush

January 24, 1848 Gold was found by James W. Marshall at Sutter's Mill in Coloma, California

49ers Gold seekers who arrived in the year 1849

1848-1855 The California Gold Rush

1000

Population of San Francisco in 1848

36,000

Population of San Francisco in 1852

300,000

Total number of gold seekers

★★★**1850** California becomes a state★★★

Marlena

While working through a unit, pause periodically to allow students to add a fact or two to the crowdsourced collection for use in developing an infographic later in the unit.

Adapting for Littles

Littles love numbers too, and they can be successful with this activity if they have some scaffolding. Collect data on a class chart while exploring books, videos, or other content together. Add the elements for the infographic on the side of their template or embed it in their drawing: stick figures, preformatted numbers, or shapes. The Noun Project add-on places line-drawing images right in Google Slides and is easy for littles to use. Littles may benefit from verbal feedback from peers until writing skills are strong enough to incorporate written feedback. Sentence frames are great for helping littles with verbal feedback and comments.

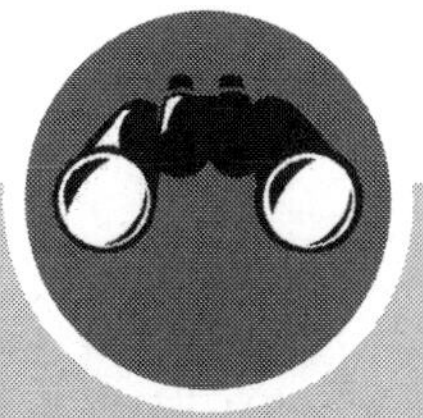

Chapter 11
Debate-It EduProtocol: Argumentative Writing

There were six weeks left before school would be out, and Coach Marlena was asked to teach a seventh-grade class for the remainder of the year. The students had developed the reputation of being a most difficult group. They had already had six substitutes, and now the principal was teaching the class. In order to try to turn the classroom around, the first thing Marlena did after taking over this class was to begin a unit on debate. Every student was engaged—not one episode of misbehavior! And she fell in love with debates and kids!

Description

Students conduct shared research before debating a topic. After the debate, students individually write their argumentative essay.

Academic Goals

- To practice research
- To develop an oral argument
- To interpret the research of others

Teacher Big Ideas

- Support struggling students with shared notes.
- Oral arguments serve as the pre-write activity and build the foundation for better writing.
- Seeing the notes of the opposing pair will help students develop better counter-arguments.
- Each student is held accountable for the final product.

Prepare for the Activity

Step 1: Create a list of topics for groups to choose from or decide on a topic for the entire class.

Step 2: Create groups of four students. Two students will argue for, and two will argue against. This group of four is now a team.

Step 3: Decide on the method or format for documenting sources according to your grade-level standards and expectations. Consider using the Group Brainstorm EduProtocol to conduct shared research.

Step 4: Create a template for students to use for collecting data.

Instructions

Step 1: All four students will keep notes in a slide deck. The two students arguing the affirmative (for) side will use the first half of the slide deck; the two students arguing the negative (against) will use the second half. (Each set of partners will need to know the other pair's findings in order to build better counter-arguments.)

(*Optional*: As students get better at debating, or for middle and high school students, allow them to work on partner slides that are not shared with the opposing teammates.)

Step 2: Each pair will curate facts with sources on slides (one source per slide, as with the Group Brainstorm EduProtocol). The more facts, the better!

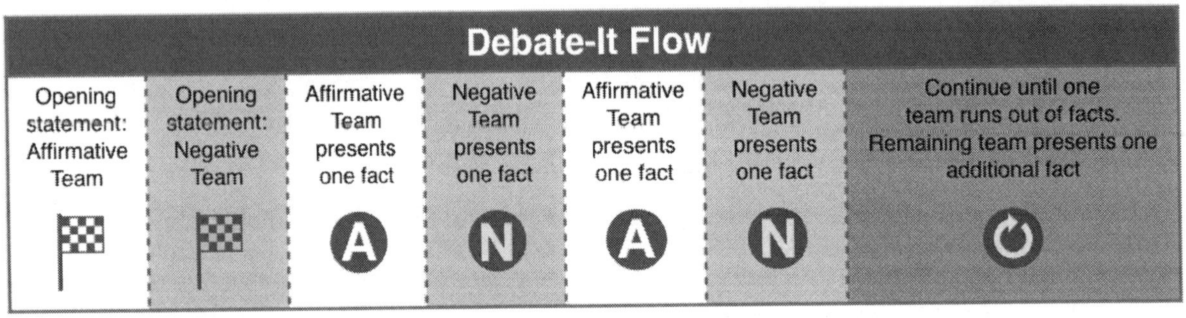

Debate-It Flow

Opening statement: Affirmative Team	Opening statement: Negative Team	Affirmative Team presents one fact	Negative Team presents one fact	Affirmative Team presents one fact	Negative Team presents one fact	Continue until one team runs out of facts. Remaining team presents one additional fact
		A	N	A	N	

Note: The affirmative team argues for and the negative team argues against.

Step 3: One pair of students will debate the opposing pair from their team using this format:

Step 4: Each student will use the shared research of the entire group of four students (two for and two against) and any notes they took during the debate to write an argumentative paper on their topic. Consider using a Debate-It EduProtocol-type document such as the one below to scaffold the writing process until students are ready to tackle argumentative writing without it.

Note: *Once a fact is used, it cannot be used by a partner again.*

Debate-It Writing EduProtocol		
Opening Paragraph • *Thesis statement* • *Postion*		
Paragraph 1	*Claim #1*	
	Evidence	
	How the evidence supports your claim	
Paragraph 1	*Claim #2*	
	Evidence	
	How the evidence supports your claim	
Paragraph 1	*Claim #3*	
	Evidence	
	How the evidence supports your claim	
Closing		

Modification

Master librarian and English teacher Brigeen Houghton uses a twist on the usual debate format in order to engage the whole class on a single topic. Students in the class form just two teams, and the whole class researches just one topic. Half the class is for, and half is against. Students record facts on three-by-five-inch cards after they conduct their research. During the debate, students from each team form a line (one team on each side of the room). Each student presents just one fact, and once that fact is used, it cannot be used again. Each team member cycles to the end of the line after presenting their argument. The team with the most facts (and thus with the best research going in) will be the winner.

Jon

Using this format as a pre-write gives students vast and in-depth exposure to different topics.

Key Points to Remember

- If students are hesitant to argue a specific side, it is helpful to remember that a great debater can defend either side of an issue. Knowing the opponent's side well is fuel for a better argument!
- Debates are generally quite formal, but formality is not necessarily important in this EduProtocol. Understanding a topic's pros and cons enough to write about them is what matters! If you wish to have your students debate formally, then you can use formal rules and structure for the debate.

English Language Learner Tip: *Encourage ELLs to participate by helping them understand the strategies used in debate. Model a mini debate, watch a video clip, or run a practice session with a silly topic to help your ELLs understand the flow and purpose.*

Adapting for Littles

As a society, we generally discourage young children from taking a stand on issues. Parents don't appreciate it when a six-year-old argues for a later bedtime, ice cream before dinner, or an item in the check-out line! Finding high-interest and acceptable topics is as much of a challenge for young debaters as it is for middle schoolers! Try looking for topics about school or scenarios on campus or at home that are of interest to your students (e.g., which new playground equipment we should purchase, which game is more fun, reasons for a later bedtime on holidays, choosing a movie, or getting an allowance).

Research one topic with the entire class. Create a list of "for" and "against" points on a shared chart. Ask students to think about what mom or dad or teacher would say and create counterpoints to that stand. Instead of debating one another, have two students role-play as a child and a parent. Then have students choose a side and write about what they might say to convince the other. Alternatively, you can leave out the writing portion and focus on using oral debate to build skills that can be used later for persuasive writing.

Chapter 12

Hero's Journey EduProtocol: Informational Writing in a Narrative Format

We do not usually think of narrative writing as informational writing, but narrative writing allows students to apply slightly informal techniques to informational writing. This protocol will extend past the personal story usually associated with this genre. The purpose of this EduProtocol is to help students think of their information writing as a story or narrative using Joseph Campbell's Hero's Journey format.

Description

In this EduProtocol, students will complete the writing task by developing an idea using a collaborative storyboard in the format of the Hero's Journey.

Academic Goals

- To use story structure to format a narrative to support informational writing
- To build writing fluency
- To cite evidence and sources in the text
- To plan and develop with a peer

Teacher Big Ideas

- Allow students time to think before writing.
- Go slow to go fast by scaffolding up from the pre-writing activity.
- Many formats can be used for constructing narrative writing, and one is not necessarily better than the other.
- This pre-write is in the form of a storyboard (so it will be shorter).

Prepare for the Activity

Step 1: Prepare a template for a comic strip or allow students to prepare their own. Label the template with the parts of the Hero's Journey and prompts for students.

- Call to Action: Identify the problem.
- Threshold: What is the background of the problem?
- Helper: Who or what is trying to change (stop, repair, replace, resolve, or heal) the course of the problem?
- Abyss: What challenge is the helper facing in his or her quest?
- Transformation: How is the helper trying to change the outcome?
- Return: What might it be like, or what is the desired result, if the helper is successful?

The Hero's Journey Story Map		
Call to Action	**Threshold**	**Helper**
Identify the problem?	What is the history or background of the problem?	Who or what agency is trying to change the course of the problem?
Abyss	**Transformation**	**Return**
What challenges is the helper facing in his/her quest?	How is the 'helper' trying to change the outcome?	What might it be like, or what is the desired result, if the 'helper' is successful?

Divide the class into partners who will work together to plan the writing. Then have each student individually write their essay based on the work they completed with their partner.

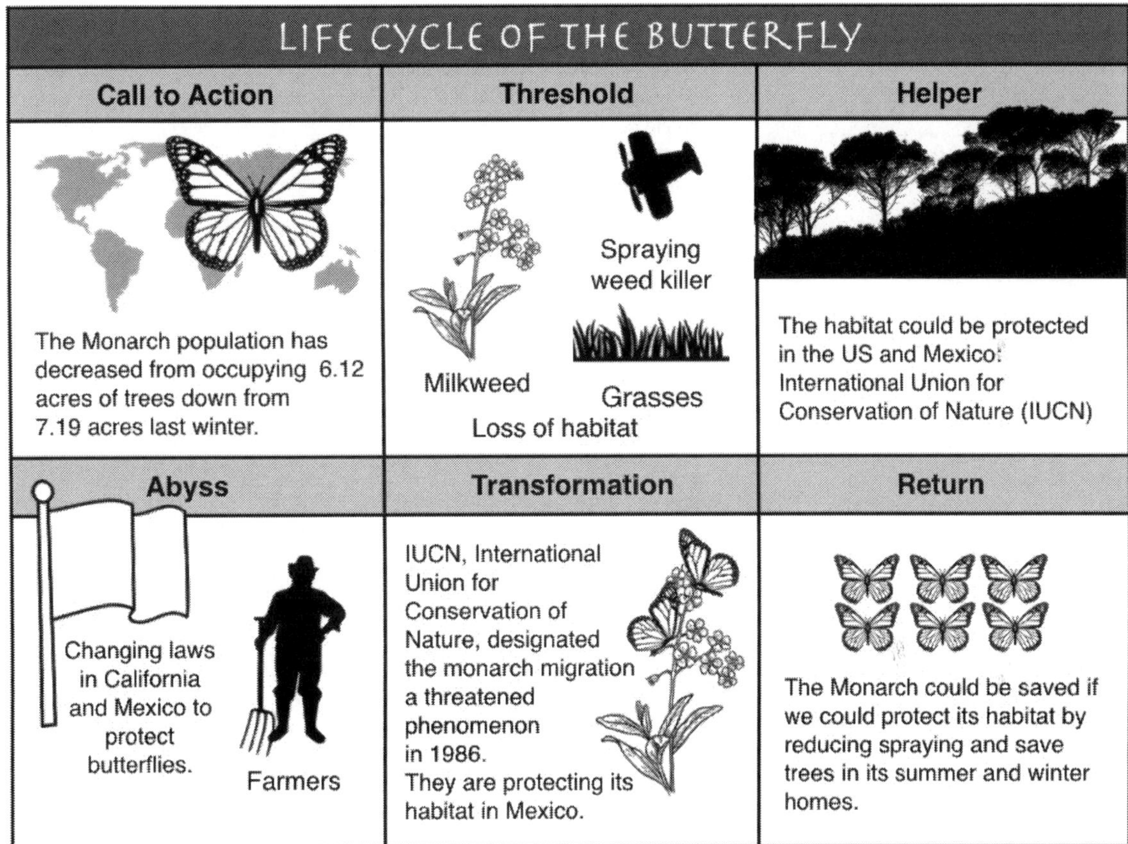

LIFE CYCLE OF THE BUTTERFLY
Call to Action
The Monarch population has decreased from occupying 6.12 acres of trees down from 7.19 acres last winter.
Threshold
Spraying weed killer
Milkweed
Grasses
Loss of habitat
Helper
The habitat could be protected in the US and Mexico: International Union for Conservation of Nature (IUCN)
Abyss
Changing laws in California and Mexico to protect butterflies.
Farmers
Transformation
IUCN, International Union for Conservation of Nature, designated the monarch migration a threatened phenomenon in 1986. They are protecting its habitat in Mexico.
Return
The Monarch could be saved if we could protect its habitat by reducing spraying and save trees in its summer and winter homes.

Tip: *Use an identical six-frame chart for students to paste their resource links into for later reference. Or use the chart as a resources menu for students to reference if you have specific sites you want them to use.*

English Language Learner Tip: *Understanding the vocabulary (call to action, threshold, helper, abyss, transformation, and return) before the lesson begins will help ELLs to engage fully.*

LIFE CYCLE OF THE BUTTERFLY		
Call to Action	**Threshold**	**Helper**
Identify the problem. https://www.usatoday.com/story/news/2018/03/06/monarch-butterfly-population-dwindled-second-straight-year-mexico/400528002/	**What is the history or background of the problem?** *https://www.monarch-butterfly.com/saving-monarchs.html*	**Who or what agency is trying to change the course of the problem?**
Abyss	**Transformation**	**Return**
What challenges is the helper facing in his/her quest?	**How is the 'helper' trying to change the outcome?**	**What might it be like, or what is the desired result, if the 'helper' is successful?** https://defenders.org/monarch-butterfly/basic-facts?s_src=3WDW1800AXXXX&s_subsrc=grant&gclid=Cj0KCQjwxN_XBRCFARIsAIufy1apFx-9_4U-sDoJD2A1kVz873rrr5o4NCkXXvdx_7n0PqHNWZKRkW0aAh1VEALw_wcB

Instructions

Step 1: (Optional) Consider showing students the Hero's Journey TED-Ed video by Matthew Winkler (http://bit.ly/EP-herosjourney) to help students understand the flow of the Hero's Journey.

Step 2: Provide the template and optional resources to the students.

Note: *Images are optional, especially if students are taking too long to find them! They are intended to help students visualize their narrative but are not required.*

Step 3: Students create their storyboard.

> ***Note:*** *The Noun Project is a great place to find black-and-white clip art. Students can save time by taking a screenshot of the image and pasting it into their work. Be sure to capture the credit on each image.*

Step 4: Students write their narrative using the images they found to illustrate key points as a guide.

Step 5: Be sure to have students cite sources as they write.

> ***English Language Learner Tip:*** *Tap into prior knowledge of the topic with video or discussion as students begin this writing project. Provide enough structure so that students are not overwhelmed and enough freedom to explore a topic from an authentic point of view.*

Key Points to Remember

- Don't overdo the prompts.
- The Hero's Journey is a guideline, not a mandate.
- Eliminate unnecessary segments, depending on the topic.
- Keep the storyboard build time very short; it is not the main writing project!

Adapting for Littles

- Simplify and shorten the activity to a beginning, middle, and end; for example, What is the problem? Who solves the problem? How do they solve the problem?
- Preformat images for students or create "libraries" on the side of your slide.
- As students find success, pull back scaffolding.

Marlena

Try to eliminate having littles retype their papers. Young students have zero patience for doing a task twice, and a final write feels a lot like a do-over when you are only six!

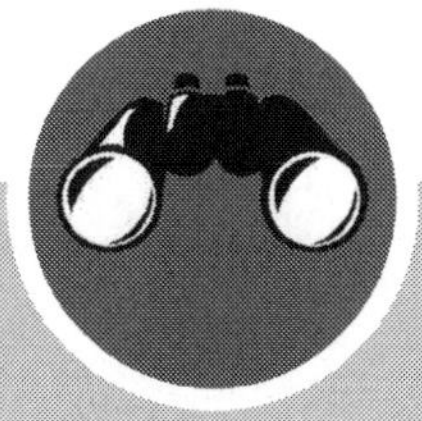

Chapter 13
The Scoop EduProtocol

Marlena has noticed in her work with at-risk students that they often have a difficult time following oral directions given to the whole class. This protocol is designed to help all students practice listening and speaking skills, including our at-risk and English learners. The name for this EduProtocol, The Scoop, is meant to help put students in the role of news reporters rushing to be the first to report a story. They must listen carefully to the details of the story as it unfolds so they can report it accurately.

Description

In The Scoop EduProtocol, students listen to a passage explaining a process or concept and then retell that process to a partner.

Academic Goals

- To listen and retell nonfiction content
- To provide feedback to a peer
- To speak fluently and clearly

Teacher Big Ideas

- All students need practice retelling what they have heard.
- Retelling uses different modalities than just listening.
- Teach students to listen to directions and instruction the first time.

Prepare for the Activity

Step 1: Find an audio passage, video clip, or an excerpt that can be read aloud. Look for course-related content or content from another area. YouTube clips of science concepts work well. Keep the passage to one minute. Short is better than long.

Instructions

Step 1: Play the passage while students listen.

Step 2: Students retell the passage to a partner while using Screencastify or Flipgrid to record. (If these programs are not available, have students focus on retelling to a partner.)

Step 3: Listen to the passage again and allow students to self-evaluate.

Key Points to Remember

- This is an oral activity
- Keep the passage to one minute.
- Resist the temptation to find *easy* content or below-grade-level content—if anything, you should step it up!
- Scaffold by slowing the YouTube video speed to begin with until students develop listening fluency.

Note: *Allowing students to use a program such as Screencastify or Flipgrid to record their retelling will allow them to listen to themselves and self-evaluate progress. This method also allows the teacher to review the video together with individual students later. If you use text-to-speech features to capture student thoughts, keep the focus on the oral retelling aspect of the experience.*

Adapting for Littles

- When adapting this activity for littles, use a more straightforward passage that is grade appropriate in content, length, and speed.
- Slow the video with reduced speed (an option in YouTube).
- Remember the listen-retell-listen method to allow students to self-evaluate for missing parts.

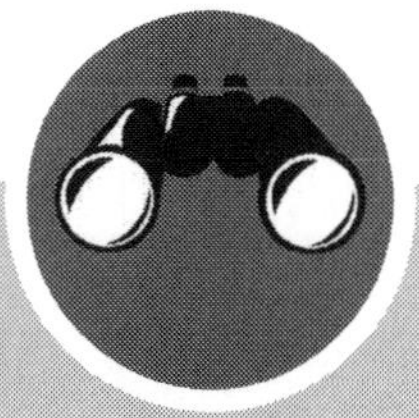

Chapter 14
Game of Quotes EduProtocol

Created by Heather Marshall (@MsMarshallCMS)

Description

This EduProtocol is unique in that it is an adaptation of the game *BYOB (Bring Your Own Book)* by Gamewright. Heather Marshall, an ELA, History, and Media Studies teacher, adapted this game for use in her classroom to encourage reading. The original *Bring Your Own Book* game is available on Amazon, and more information is available about the game on bringyourownbook.com. The basic idea of this game is that a prompt is chosen, such as *a phrase that could inspire revolt* or *a sentence in a fortune cookie,* and students search their book for the best response.

Heather recalls, "I got the idea in a comic book store when I came across this card game called *BYOB (Bring Your Own Book)*. I bought it, took it home, and immediately went to work trying to adapt it for the classroom. I thought this game would be a fun way to get students' eyes on text. I think I am the one who is really winning this game, though, because not only are my students reading, they are also getting their classmates interested in new books! I highly recommend this game!"

Academic Goals

- To get kids excited about reading
- To find textual evidence quickly
- To improve recall of read material

Teacher Big Ideas

- Move beyond surface-level questions by tying in literary devices and themes from class studies.
- Reinforce at-home reading.
- Silent reading alone has little instructional value, so balance appropriately within your overall curriculum.

Jon

This approach to silent reading is a GAME-Changer. We have heard many anecdotes of students being energized in their independent reading. Kevin Sinclair has had his students start tagging their books with Post-It Notes in case a quote might be useful in class the next day. We have also heard of a student who reads below grade level, but when on a four-game winning streak of Games of Quotes contests, imagine how energized that student is about reading!

English Language Learner Tip: *Provide time for ELLs to work in pairs to find quotes. Processing information in their native language will deepen the connection and the learning.*

Prepare for the Activity

Create a slide deck with prompts for the questions. Use the *BYOB (Bring Your Own Book)* game for prompt ideas or download some from the bringyourownbook.com website.

Instructions

Step 1: Students read quietly for eight to ten minutes.

Step 2: After eight to ten minutes of reading, reveal the prompt for round one.

Step 3: The students flip through the pages of their books looking for a good response to the prompt. Once a student says, "Got it!" the rest of the class has two minutes to lock in their answer.

Step 4: Students share their responses in table groups and vote on a winner. The table group winners share their answers one-by-one. It's ok not to vote on a winner or to allow students to share the best response from each table group.

Key Points to Remember

- Have fun but go deeper into standards and themes for the prompts.
- Finding prompts in their books will reinforce curricular goals.
- Students will want to flag potential quotes. Say, "Yes!"

Adaptations

- Use this scavenger hunt concept in math, history, or other content areas. Create your own cards related to your subject area.

Adapting for Littles

Keep prompts child friendly so students can relate to them. Also use prompts from the content so the quotes they find support the main ideas and goals of instruction. There's no need to choose winners; you can set it up so everyone wins! Try having the whole class read the same book so the same quotes are accessible to all learners.

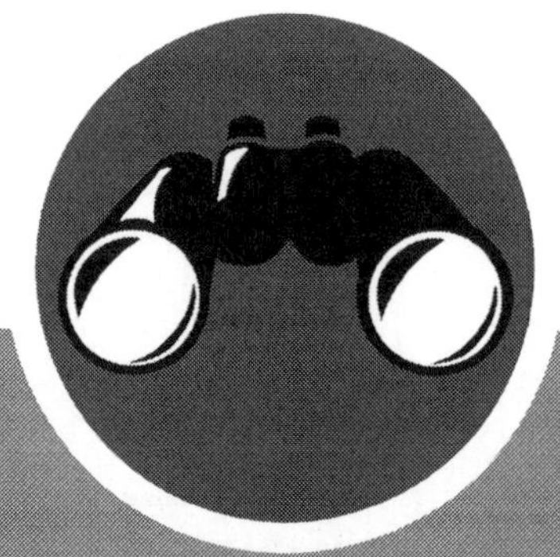

SECTION 3
Remixing and Revising

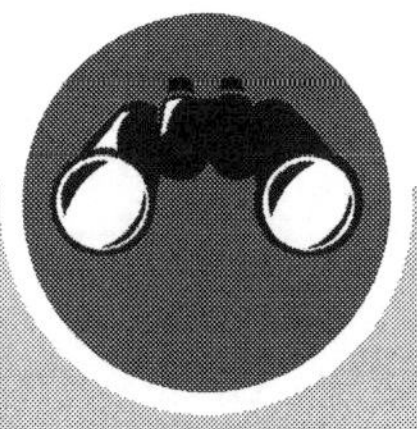

Chapter 15
Open Pedagogy

Thousands of candles can be lit from a single candle, and the life of the candle will not be shortened. Happiness never decreases by being shared.

—Gautama Buddha (attributed), Sutta Nipata

When we design EduProtocols, we intend to strike an instructional balance: We design lessons that will be used over and over by students to facilitate technology integration into classrooms while also inspiring teachers to be the very best instructional leaders they can. Then we encourage educators to take our lesson frames and adapt them and share alike.

This practice of sharing teaching resources is called Open Pedagogy. We did not make up that term; it has been around for a while and is often used in relationship to Open Educational Resources (OER), which are textbooks that are free and available for teachers and students. Many colleges are promoting Open Pedagogy in an attempt to reduce the ever-growing cost of textbooks for students, but there are also several excellent OER collections available for K–12 education such as Khan Academy, Power My Learning, Big History Project, NROC Math Project, and Educurious. Many of these sites are funded by foundations in order to provide equitable access to quality educational materials.

OERs are rich learning and teaching materials that are . . .

- Free to access
- Free to reuse
- Free to revise
- Free to remix
- Free to redistribute

These five principles of OERs are the foundation of the resources used with open pedagogy.

Jon

OERs have the main advantage of being produced by folks with passion and vision. Many corporately designed products lack that soul.

EduProtocols as Open Pedagogy

We call the EduProtocols Open Pedagogy because while the EduProtocols are copyrighted material and should not be published elsewhere without our permission, we *do* encourage you to use them freely in your classrooms and to reuse, revise, remix, and share with your colleagues in person and on social media. Take time to get to know them. Understand the principles underlying the EduProtocols and try some in the classroom. Learn the structures of the protocol you want to use, and when you're ready, find natural ways to adapt and modify it to meet the learning needs of your students. Don't be afraid to try someone else's methods. Kids are kids, so what works with one class will probably work with another! You can join the EduProtocol community on Twitter and share what you've used with the hashtag #EduProtocols so others can use, share, and remix your work! Many of the best EduProtocol ideas have come from remixing the work of others.

Giving Credit to the Work of Others

Use the Creative Commons Attribution-Share-Alike citation when remixing and re-sharing EduProtocols that were created by someone else. You may use, remix, tweak, and build upon them as you wish, but make sure you give credit to the creator, and allow new users the same freedom to adapt your work as well.

Naming EduProtocols

Give significantly redesigned EduProtocols a new identity by renaming them. Doing so keeps students from getting confused about the processes involved in a given protocol. If, for instance, the Cyber Sandwich has been significantly redesigned but retains its name, students may not realize they are embarking on a different learning activity when you announce, "Next up is a Cyber Sandwich." They will most likely transfer knowledge from a prior session of that EduProtocol to this one. EduProtocols are intended to reduce student stress and affective filters, and having different names for different variations is a good step toward that goal.

What is a "significant redesign"? Adding a Flipgrid to the reflection portion of the Cyber Sandwich is an excellent idea if it meets curricular goals; however, it is not a significant redesign and therefore does not warrant a new name. Removing the Venn diagram and replacing it with three new steps that are entirely different from those in the original Cyber Sandwich would be a significant enough redesign to justify a new name.

When Kevin Feramisco (@theteachingjedi) and his students blended the Iron Chef EduProtocol and the Frayer EduProtocol into one activity, the natural choice for a new name was the Iron Chef Frayer EduProtocol. Combining the names of the protocols points the students to two activities they already know and lets them easily deduce what the new activity will look like: an Iron Chef using a Frayer!

Let the Fun Begin!

Educators share their remixed EduProtocol creations with us all the time, and we love seeing how teachers are using them to engage students! The following chapters contain a few notable remixes of the EduProtocols we presented in *The EduProtocol Field Guide, Book One*. If you plan to implement these variations, we suggest you begin with the versions in the original field guide. Once you understand those, branch out into some of these variations. We hope the following twists on our favorite EduProtocols will help inspire you to create your own! If you're inspired to create new variations, please share them with us using #EduProtocols on Twitter, or you can use the contact form available on the EduProtocols.com website to reach Jon or Marlena.

Call to Action

Seasoned User

If you have been using EduProtocols in your classroom or with students, share some of your iterations and ideas on Twitter for others to enjoy.

New to EduProtocols?

If you are new to using EduProtocols, check out what other teachers are doing at EduProtocols.com (look for samples on the templates pages) or on Twitter with #EduProtocols.

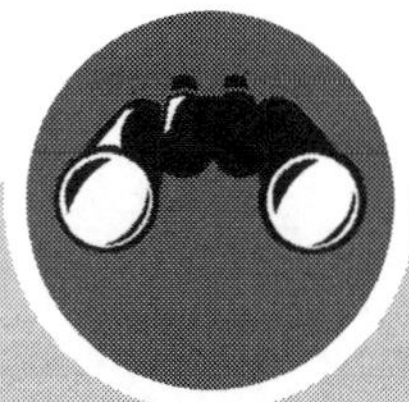

Chapter 16
Iron Chef EduProtocol Remixes

Iron Chef Frayer EduProtocol
Adapted by Kevin Feramisco (@theteachingjedi) along with his students

Description

The Iron Chef Frayer is run as an Iron Chef EduProtocol, except that a Frayer is used instead of a blank slide. Students in groups of four to six complete the activity and then present their slides to the class in the fashion of the Iron Chef EduProtocol.

Assign one to four Frayers per student based on ability and grade level. After the Iron Chef-style presentations, the completed Iron Chef Frayer slide deck becomes a complete vocabulary/concept study guide for each student.

Preparing for the Activity

Prepare four Frayer template slides per student for each group of four students (sixteen total slides).

Instructions

In groups of four, students complete the Frayers in the fashion of the Iron Chef EduProtocol as presented in *The EduProtocol Field Guide, Book One*. Have each student complete one to four Frayers within this slide deck so four students together complete up to sixteen Frayer slides.

Marlena

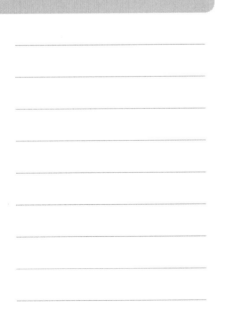

Find the complete directions for the Iron Chef EduProtocol and the presentation style for the Iron Chef in *The EduProtocol Field Guide, Book One.*

Adapting for Littles

Can our youngest students do a Frayer? Indeed they can! Try using an LMS or Google Classroom to make the sharing process smoother for young students. Also allow students to use images in the example and non-example fields of the Frayer to speed up their workflow and allow a visual representation. It requires a higher Depth of Knowledge (DOK) level of two to infer or three to construct and/or draw conclusions in order to find fitting images. (This is true for older students as well!)

Iron Chef Frayer

Definition

Characteristics

Word

Example

Non-example

Iron Chef Flash Readers Theater EduProtocol

Adapted by Katie Baker (@KtBkr4)

The Iron Chef Flash Project Protocol is a way to infuse creativity, ingenuity, and collaboration into a performance-based project. Whereas in the original Iron Chef protocol students use a slide template to work collaboratively on a jigsaw-type project, students using the Iron Chef Flash Project Protocol are provided with key ingredients and directions to quickly create either a screencast, a recorded performance, or a project to show what they know about specific content. This is a fun, community-building activity that is completed after formative assessments and prior to summative assessments. The Iron Chef Flash Project Protocol can be replicated with any content in any subject area as a way to let students show what they know.

Marlena

Remixing EduProtocols is a great way to expand the EduProtocol that your students know with something new. Mixing it up will hold the interest of your students!

Description

Students use the structure of Iron Chef in an open-project format to demonstrate understanding of literature or of other topics studied.

Academic Goals

- To demonstrate understanding of concepts
- To communicate ideas in a clear and concise manner
- To make choices as an artist
- To practice reflective thinking skills

Teacher Big Ideas

- The Iron Chef Flash Project Protocol is an effective review activity to be completed after formative assessments and prior to summative assessments. This protocol also works well for building community and strengthening students' interpersonal skills.

- Other than providing the key ingredients for the Iron Chef Flash Project Protocol, monitoring student progress during the class period, and determining the workflow for uploading and sharing videos/projects, the teacher should allow students freedom to figure out how to create their video/project on their own.
- Teachers should not feel the need to score videos/projects created with the Iron Chef Flash Project Protocol. The emphasis is not on a grade but on the process of collaboration and creation in a short timeframe. Students who can create a finished video/project should be lauded for their efforts, and those who struggled should be encouraged to reflect and pinpoint areas for improvement.
- Develop quick timelines and keep students moving.

Prepare for the Activity

Step 1: Determine the key ingredients: What are the three must-haves for students to include in their video/project? Add a fourth ingredient that is not included in the material. This fourth "Iron Chef secret ingredient" should be something unrelated (even silly) that the students need to determine how to incorporate into their video/project.

- English Language Arts: For a Readers' Theater experience, determine the text and allow students to choose ten to twelve individual lines from the scene/chapter to create a condensed version of the scene.
- Music Classes: Determine the pieces from which students will pull excerpts to create a condensed performance.
- Science Class: Determine the subject matter and edtech tools with which students will create a "show what we know" video.
- Math Class: Determine the formulas, mathematical concepts, and edtech tools with which students will create a "show what we know" video.

Step 2: Determine the workflow for students to record, upload, and share videos/projects with the class.

- If using the Google Suite or a Learning Management System (LMS), provide students with specific directions for uploading and sharing their videos/projects with the class.
    - Google Form collection of links?
    - Upload videos to YouTube/Vimeo?
- If allowing students to use edtech tools, create a choice board of tools from which students will select to make their project.

Step 3: Create slides or a document that includes the ingredients and directions for uploading/sharing videos/projects with the class.

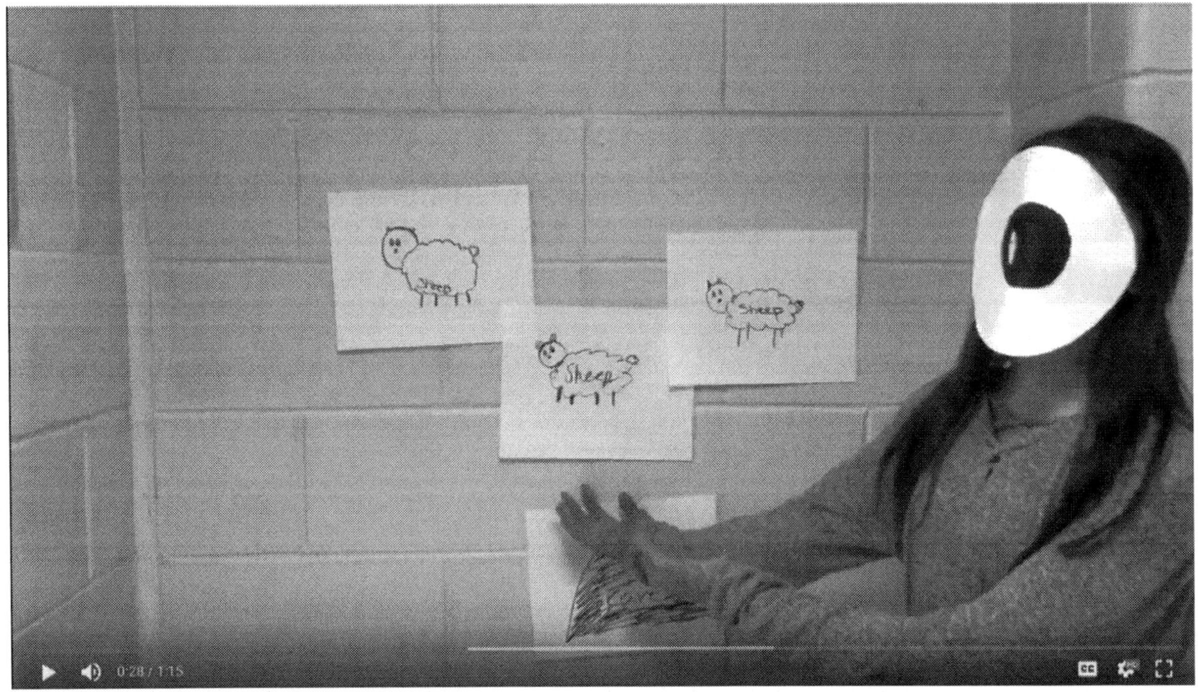

The Iron Chef Flash Readers' Theater Project, Cyclops Episode of *The Odyssey*, uses simple props.

Instructions

Step 1: (Three minutes) Students get into groups. Groups must have at least one person with a smartphone, tablet, Chromebook, or other mobile technology. Students may use personal or school-provided devices.

Step 2: (Fifteen to twenty minutes) Determine how to incorporate the ingredients and content. Write a script, prototype, or storyboard of what will be captured in the video/project.

Step 3: (Fifteen minutes) Determine how to perform and record the video or create the project within the class period.

Step 4: (Five minutes) Share the video/project with the teacher and class and view other students' videos/projects.

Step 5: (Five minutes) Write a reflection on the creation and performance process. The reflection can be completed at home or outside of class. Have students answer the following questions:

- How did you decide what to do?
- Why did you make the choices you made?
- What can you do to make your project "better"?
- What do you still need to do to complete it?
- What skills did you use/learn during the creation process?
- How does your project show what you know?

Key Points to Remember

- Keep an eye on the time or use a YouTube timer and remind students that the video/project must be completed within the class period. This is a QUICK video/project to show what they know.
- The Iron Chef Flash Video/Project is a fun activity that focuses on the creative process. No grade needed for this protocol!

Iron Chef Flash projects can take many forms.

Adaptations

- Think how you might use this format in the math classroom. Jeremiah Rouch has students show the math solution to a problem four different ways, each method on a different slide.

Adapting for Littles

- Provide elementary students with the necessary hardware to create the video/project. Remember that it will take time for younger students to learn what to do. Consider a practice run recording something short and fun the day before. Programs such as SeeSaw can be used to manage recording.
- The teacher may need to handle the process for saving the video/project to the class's online repository.

- Slow the project with a two-day process:
    - Day 1: Plan the video/project
    - Day 2: Create and share the video/project
- Consider filming all the "skits" as they are presented to the class.

Iron Chef In-the-Field EduProtocol

Turning observations into visual and data-driven presentations is a vital component of occupations that require communicating results and research to clients and investors. In this protocol, we strive to position students as storytellers of this information as they construct and report findings to their peers.

Description

Use Iron Chef for collecting field data! Each person in the group has a data point to monitor, such as counting, measuring, or weighing. Students may need to take a few notes on paper while they are away from computers and then transfer those data once they return to the classroom.

Each student builds one of the four slides with their results and then presents their slides to their group or class in a cohesive presentation in the fashion of the Iron Chef EduProtocol.

Prepare for the Activity

Prepare a template for students. For upper grades and high school, allow students to work on a blank slide deck to allow more freedom when presenting data in a visual format.

Instructions

Deploy the Iron Chef as described in *The EduProtocol Field Guide, Book One* with a few modifications. After the students build their individual slides, allow a ten-minute huddle for students to strategize their presentation message based on the findings as a whole: five minutes to review the data in each slide and five minutes to decide on a unified message for the presentation. Eventually students will be able to complete this step as they collect data and work on their slides and will use the formal five-minute huddle to firm up their plans.

Adapting for Littles

Younger students may also need to take a few notes on paper while they are away from the computers, so they will need a little time to translate their notes upon return as well. Avoid long and arduous copying of prior work for younger students. Try drawing in the field and then translating that image into words on the computer. Break up this activity so that there are small bursts of computer work instead of having them translate hours of a fieldwork at a time onto the computers. Littles will be less effective with the ten-minute huddle, so consider working this in as they gain experience.

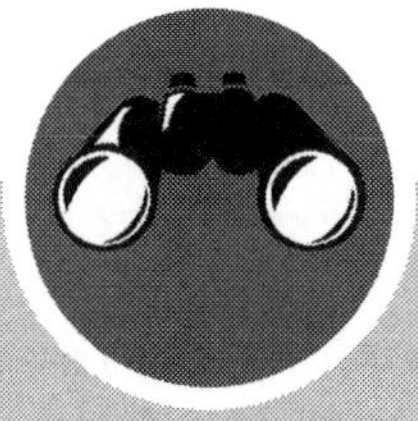

Chapter 17
Cyber Sandwich Remixes

Cyber Sandwich has proven to be a versatile tool for the classroom, and teachers have embraced its simplicity for comprehension and student engagement. This modification of the Cyber Sandwich EduProtocol is just one example of how it might be expanded to support students as a pre-writing activity.

Cyber Sandwich Argumentative

Having adequate time for processing is vital for understanding. In this Cyber Sandwich modification, we are going to extend one topic over three days to allow students to develop a deeper understanding of the pros and cons of a given topic using the Venn diagram in the Cyber Sandwich. There is a calculated change in the normal timing of this EduProtocol intended to allow for a deeper dive into a specific topic.

Description

Students use two Cyber Sandwiches to explore the pros and cons of a given topic and then write individual essays using the notes they created through the Cyber Sandwich activity.

Prepare for the Activity

Prepare a Cyber Sandwich template for two rounds so the pros and cons of the topic are together in one slide deck. (The Cyber Sandwich template may be found at EduProtocols.com.) Two Cyber Sandwich templates back-to-back are useful for facilitating the complexity of this activity for all grade levels.

Instructions

Day 1: Student partners use a Cyber Sandwich to read and discuss an article in support of the chosen topic. Keep to the 10, 10, 10 flow of the original Cyber Sandwich:

- 10 minutes to read
- 10 minutes to pair-share/Venn diagram
- 10 minutes to quick-write a summary

Day 2: Student partners use a Cyber Sandwich to read and discuss an article against the same topic as presented on Day 1. Remember to stick to the 10, 10, 10 flow of Cyber Sandwich.

Day 3: Students write their essay per the rigor dictated by grade-level standards and school expectations.

Adapting for Littles

Use the three-day approach for littles and keep the content at grade level. Consider working through the writing portion of this activity as a group until students know what to expect. Use story books and short reads as source material.

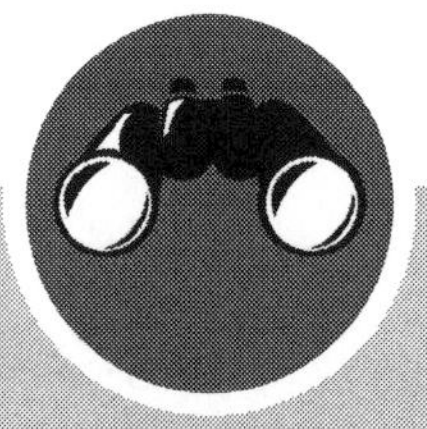

Chapter 18
The Fast and Curious EduProtocol Remixes

Class Tracking in The Fast and Curious

Contributed by Nichole Chun (@learnswithzeal)

As teacher and blogger of *Zealous EdTech-Zealous Learning*, Nichole Chun, discovered, tracking progress in The Fast and Curious as a whole class is one way to build culture and community among students. We offer this tip not so much as an adaptation of an EduProtocol, but as a valuable addition. Consider using a class chart or some other method to consistently track progress and growth of the whole group. Enlist the whole class as you attempt to break class scores and keep the learning going strong! Back in the day, we would have called this cooperative learning!

Jon

If you create a new remix, share it back with us on Twitter at #EduProtocols! We can't wait to see what you cook up!

Self-Paced Fast and Curious EduProtocol

Adapted by Ben Cogswell (@cogswell_ben)

Description

Ben Cogswell shifted the responsibility, control, and ownership of math fact mastery to students by automating their practice using the Fast and Curious EduProtocol. Students track their progress in a chart that is shared with the teacher.

Prepare for the Activity

Make a quiz (or find suitable quizzes in Quizizz or another quiz program) and share the quiz as "homework" so students can choose the link without the teacher running the quiz in real time.

Create a tracking method for the quizzes and share that document with students. In this model, students must score 80 percent five times for each level before moving on to the next. Students are allowed to start with the math fact of their choosing.

WARNING! This challenge is only for those ready to become a true **MASTER OF MULTIPLICATION!**
To become a master takes time and dedication.
To do so, you must achieve **100%, perfect score**, on each level, **5 times.**
Can you master them all?

DIRECTIONS: You may choose which multiplication facts to start on. Copy the game code next to the facts and go to **QUIZIZZ.COM/JOIN/.**
When you achieve 100%, write the date in the same row as the fact completed under the first star. Repeat the process until you can master each level 5 times. You may skip around as you may like.

CLICK HERE FOR QUIZIZZ

MULTIPLICATION FACTS	Game Code	Achieved Mastery ★	Achieved Mastery ★★	Achieved Mastery ★★★	Achieved Mastery ★★★★	Achieved Mastery ★★★★★
1s	738983					
2s	732872					
3s	556638					
4s	600130					
5s	467477					
6s	467890					
7s	833101					
8s	722672					
9s	939945					
10s	373802					
BOSS LEVEL	278302					

Quizizz Multiplication Collection @cogswell_ben

Adapting for Littles

Once littles are ready to practice math facts in this format, train them to record their percentages in a doc or spreadsheet, record-keeping page, or pocket chart. Help them learn to reflect upon their progress at intervals.

Chapter 19
Mini-Report EduProtocol Remix

Storyboard Story

Adapted by Adam Moler (@moler3031)

Description

Adam created this adaptation of the Mini-Report EduProtocol with his seventh- and eighth-grade history students to help them visualize history!

Prepare for the Activity

Students complete a mini-report using a topic of study. In Adam's class, students were learning about life in the Roman Empire.

Provide a format for students to create their storyboard. Adam used Storyboard That and Pixton, but you can make wonderful storyboards using Google Drawing or any other graphic program that allows students to manipulate images and add speech bubbles.

Instructions

Students complete a mini-report on the topic of study. They then create, frame by frame, the dialogue their characters will use in the comic strip. Once the dialogue is written, students create the comic strip using their graphics program.

Adapting for Littles

Provide a frame for the dialogue in three or four boxes. Provide a matching template for the comic strips if you are using a program such as Google Drawing. Consider providing images and dialogue bubbles on the side of the workspace so students can use drag-and-drop to form their comic strips. We do not usually have students transfer handwritten work to typed text, but this is one instance where a pre-write dialogue on paper may be productive for littles.

Chapter 20
BookaKucha EduProtocol Remix

BookaKucha Bingo

Adapted by Carly Sturm (@SturmToSA)

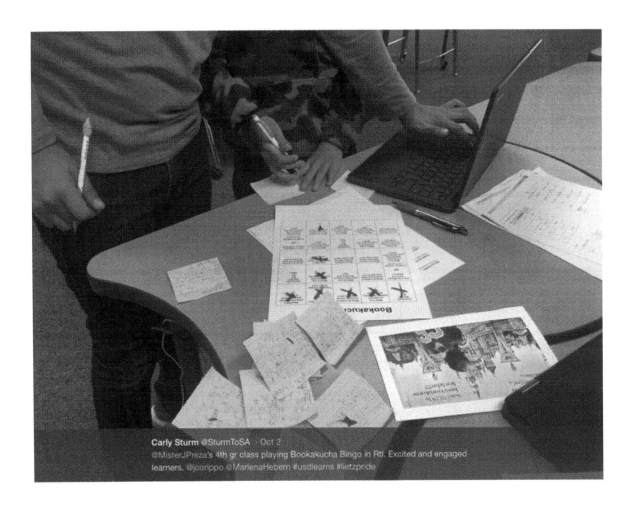

Carly Sturm @SturmToSA · Oct 2
@MisterJPreza's 4th gr class playing Bookakucha Bingo in RtI. Excited and engaged learners. @jcorippo @MarlenaHebern #usdlearns #lietzpride

BookaKucha Bingo was created by Carly Strum, Instructional Support ToSA, as an adaptation to BookaKucha. In this protocol, students choose their own prompt for their book by using a bingo board. This way they are provided choice while working through a variety of comprehension activities.

Instructions

Provide a bingo board for each student to track progress. Be sure you spend time teaching the different responses before asking students to work independently on prompts. The bingo board may have as few as three items repeated three times, or it may be more complicated, like the one shown below.

Adapting for Littles

Littles can tackle the bingo board as well. Make sure they fully understand how to do each of the responses you choose to include on the bingo card and then slowly introduce additions to the board as the class is exposed to and masters each prompt. Even two items repeated several times on a bingo board is fun for littles. Or try a class bingo board and work through it as a whole team!

BookaKucha Bingo			
Somebody... Wanted... But... So... Then...	Describe a character in detail and use textual evidence.	What are 3 wishes a character would make and why?	Tell about a dangerous situation for the character and how that character handled it.
Tell about one aha moment the character has had in the story.	What are 3 lessons that the main character has learned and why?	Describe 3 settings in the story and why they are important.	Describe one funny situation your character has encountered.
What is a moral lesson your character learned?	Describe a 'sticky situation' and what happened as a result.	Describe a character in detail and use textual evidence.	What is one thing the character would never do and why?
What is a lesson your character has had that has changed him or her?	Describe an event, situation, or word that has been repeated in the story. What is the significance?	What is one conflict in the story and one possible solution?	What are 3 lessons that the main character has learned and why?

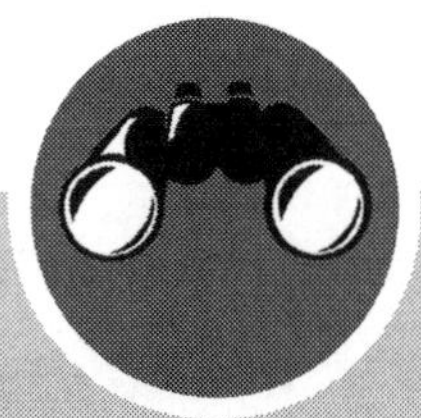

Chapter 21
Comma pARTS EduProtocol

Comma pARTS

Created by Nupur Sethi (@nupurssethi)

8 pARTS and Sentence pARTS were introduced in *The EduProtocol Field Guide, Book One*, and teachers immediately began adapting the protocol for a wide variety of uses. This newest version by English teacher Nupur Sethi is one of our favorites. In this version, Nupur has her students work through all of the possible ways commas can be used in sentences as they write about a picture. They then write a story about the picture using at least six of the sentences they created.

As you try 8 pARTS, Sentence pARTS, Comma pARTS, or a version you create yourself, remember that repetition is so very important in this activity. Begin as a whole class making shared sentences and work toward independence after a week or so. Use the activity as a whole so students learn all of it at once. Repeat until students can execute the activity quickly and accurately. It is ok if this protocol takes more than one day to complete, but the ultimate goal should be completion within twenty minutes or so. If you find yourself correcting these at night, you are doing it incorrectly! Provide resources so students can check their own answers, and then provide general feedback to point them in the right direction. Keep the workload on the kids, not on yourself.

Jon

Free templates are available at EduProtocols.com for all the pARTS protocols.

Comma pARTS		
Rule 1 Commas after day & year in a date, after day and date, if sentence doesn't end- comma after the date	**Write a paragraph about the picture using at least SIX different rules.**	
Rule 2 Comma between city or state, between city, between city and country, street address, place a comma after the state or country if it appears before the end of the sentence		**Rule 3** Comma at the end of quotations, after the person's name +verb. If quotation is split- comma after the first part
Rule 4 Comma to set off introductory words	**Rule 5** Comma to set off interrupters in a sentence	**Rule 6** Commas after a noun of direct address
Rule 7 Commas to clarify	**Rule 8** Between two more adjectives unless a color or number	**Rule 9** Comma to invert a name
Rule 10 Before the conjunction	**Rule 11** Comma after the three or more series, after phrases in a series	**Rule 12** Set off an appositive

Adapting for Littles

Younger students can easily tackle sentence parts. Simply shorten the types of sentences so they aligned with or slightly above grade-level standards. It may begin as simply as a list, city and state separation, or a comma before a coordinating conjunction (and, but, for, or, nor, so, yet).

Rule 1: Write a sentence with a city and state.
Example: Rick sits on the beach in Big Sur, California.

Rule 2: Write a sentence that lists three things.
Example: Sammy likes bugs, butterflies, and bees.

Rule 3: Write a sentence that uses a coordinating conjunction (and, but, or, so, yet).

Example: Run fast, or you will miss the bus!

Little Comma pARTS	
Directions: **Be sure to use commas in each sentence that you write about the picture.**	
Rule 1 **Write a sentence with a city and state.**	
Rule 2 **Write a sentence that lists 3 things.**	
Rule 12 **Write a sentence that uses a coordinating conjunction: and, but, or, so, yet.**	

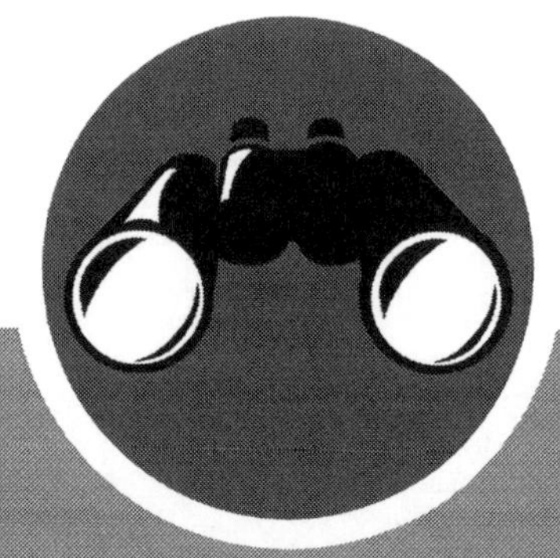

SECTION 4

Guide to Deeper Understanding

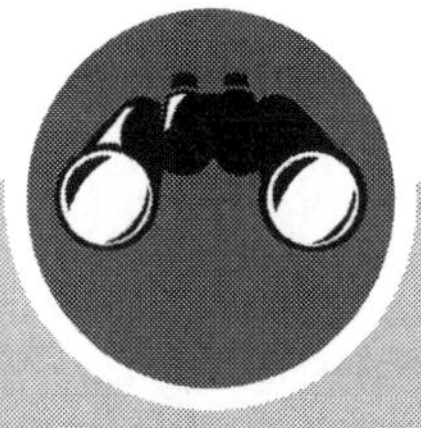

Chapter 22
The Art of Stacking

Gravity is the only "glue" that holds these structures in equilibrium.

—Michael Grab, stone balancing artist

We have learned how to use a protocol for classroom instruction to reduce the cognitive load on students and allow them to refocus on the content instead of the task. But what happens when the content becomes more complicated or longer than one EduProtocol can handle?

One way to organize classroom instruction that is too lengthy for one EduProtocol is to stack one EduProtocol on top of another, like rocks balanced in a tower, to allow students to tackle a longer or more complicated stretch of the curriculum in segments.

Jon

Rocks stacked like this are called "trail dux." Dux: to go first or lead the way. Another name for them is "cairns." Cairn: a landmark. (Sorry. My teacher brain couldn't help pointing this out.)

Stacks may be completed within one period, or they may take more than one day. Keep pacing in mind as students work through the stack—just the right amount of time for the right amount of content!

Let the Stacking Begin!

Using an old favorite, Cyber Sandwich, let's take a look at how the stacking process works.

Background: Cyber Sandwich is an EduProtocol in which students read a passage using the annotation methods taught and practiced in their particular classroom while also taking bullet-point notes. Students work with a partner to Venn diagram the bullet points, looking for similarities and differences or contrasting points of view. Then, using new knowledge and insights gleaned from the discussion, each student writes their summarizing paragraph.

Directions for the Cyber Sandwich EduProtocol are on page 10.

To use the stacking concept with Cyber Sandwich, use an extended reading passage or several passages related to the topic. Students will complete two or more Cyber Sandwiches in a row. The Cyber Sandwich Argumentative EduProtocol is an example of stacking Cyber Sandwiches.

To prepare the Stacked Cyber Sandwich, find a reading passage that is long enough to be broken up and can sustain students through two or more cycles of moving from one part to the next. Alternatively, you can use two or more related passages that build on a topic or concept. After completing one cycle, move on to the next section and repeat the process as many times as needed.

Use a timer to keep everyone on track. There are times when students work best at their own pace, but the Cyber Sandwich EduProtocol is designed to keep a group or class moving along at the same pace.

Let's look at another example of stacking, this time using the EduProtocol Sketch and Tell. In Sketch and Tell, students read the provided content, create a visual representation of their understanding, and share it with their peers. As in the previous example, you should find natural breaks in the literature or content to give students an opportunity to pause and create their visual representation. These breaks in the reading will allow for short bursts of activity, lasting from five to ten minutes, giving students enough time to pause, think about their reading and comprehension, and create a visual representation of their understanding thus far. They will then cement that understanding by sharing and explaining their thinking with a peer.

English Language Learner Tip: *Learning a new language is hard work. Allow students the gift of familiarity that the EduProtocols provide and scaffold in strong ELL strategies such as intentional partner groups, pre-teaching vocabulary, curriculum walkthroughs, and sentence starters.*

Directions for the Sketch and Tell EduProtocol are on page 25.

Call to Action

Many of the EduProtocols are built to stack! As students get faster, the master teacher will add technical details and skills to increase the cognitive load and *deepen rigor* for students *instead* of switching to a new activity. The EduProtocol then becomes the tool, not the main focus.

Choose an EduProtocol you have used in the past with your students and try stacking with some of your content. Adjust the EduProtocol as needed as you strive to find the right assignment length for the attention span of your students. Reflect on how it worked and make notes for next time.

Jon

Teach students to finish by curating five Cyber Sandwiches into a five-paragraph report!

Marlena

We do that by providing just the right amount of content for the right amount of time!

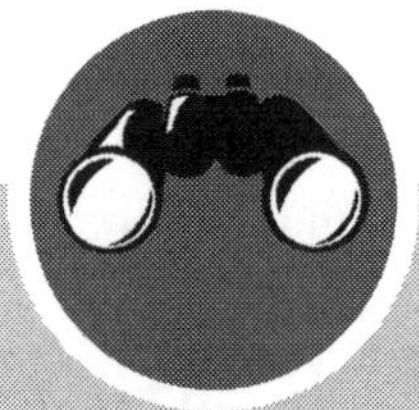

Chapter 23
EduProtocol Smashing

I am desperate for change—now—not in eight years or twelve years, but right now. We don't have time to wait.

—Michelle Obama

Some EduProtocols are naturally more suitable for stacking; others are more suitable for smashing! Just as a monster truck can take on a row of cars by approaching one at a time, we can move through the curriculum by proceeding through one protocol at a time.

In Number Mania, for example, students build a conceptual understanding of a significant event by using numbers to explore or research a topic. Number Mania does not necessarily lend itself to repetitive short bursts, so we recommend nesting it within a series of unlike protocols; for example, start with Sketch and Tell, then proceed through our old favorite, Cyber Sandwich, and culminate the learning series with Number Mania.

Sketch and Tell → Cyber Sandwich → Number Mania

All you need are two EduProtocols to begin smashing.

Directions for the Number Mania EduProtocol are on page 55.

EduProtocol Smashing is the process of moving through the curriculum by mixing two or more EduProtocols in a series in order to accommodate more complicated or more protracted curriculum tasks in a series of lessons that come together to form a unit.

Getting started with EduProtocol Smashing is easy! Simply master a minimum of any two EduProtocols individually, then combine them into one smash.

Marlena

I like to think of Smashing like a Pac-Man game, crunching our way through the content.

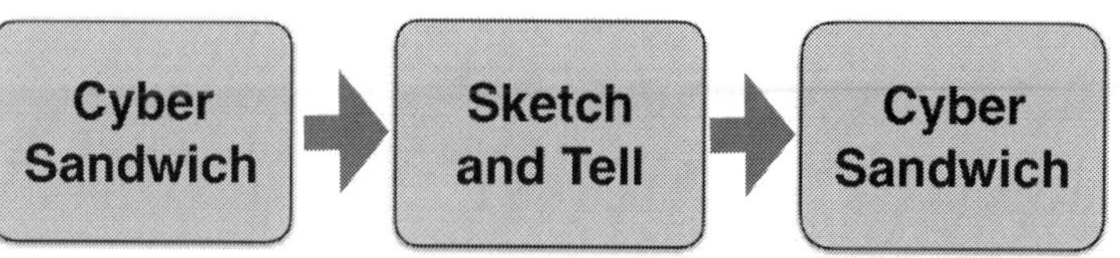

Two or more protocols in any order can create an effective smash.

Marlena

Form follows function, so how many times each EduProtocol repeats in a smash should be dictated by the content covered.

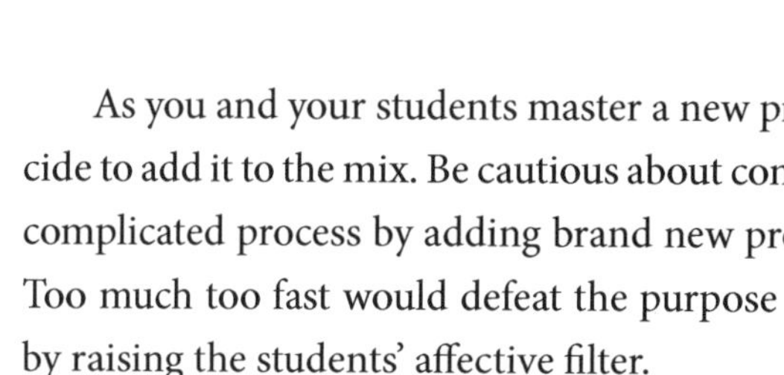

As you and your students master a new protocol, you may decide to add it to the mix. Be cautious about complicating an already complicated process by adding brand new protocols into the row. Too much too fast would defeat the purpose of the EduProtocols by raising the students' affective filter.

We want EduProtocols to slow the technology curve in order to speed up the curriculum learning curve. Prematurely adding brand-new protocols to the smash has the potential to defeat this essential purpose.

Jon

Nothing spells panic like too much too fast. Kids will shut down and reject the EduProtocol rollout. Keep it light and quick with low chances of failure.

Call to Action

You have probably tried Cyber Sandwich or another EduProtocol at this point. Add another to your repertoire. Once you and your students feel comfortable, smash them together!

Reflect on the process. How did you do with the new combination? How did your students do? What might you need to adjust for next time? Repeat this exact smash with new content to allow your students time to become more familiar with this new process before trying a new combination.

Jon

We have to lose some time in the beginning to gain time in the end. It is not an "if" but a "when;" however, by artfully developing high-tempo, low-fail activities, we can make the "lost" time just the bare minimum, literally two to three reps. The payoff is having kids who are agile, comfortable, and capable the rest of the year. Priceless.

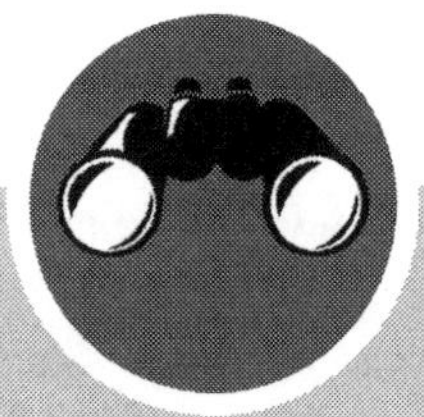

Chapter 24
Why EduProtocols Work

The mass of a body is a measure of its energy content.

—Albert Einstein

Teaching is more intuitive for some than for others, and while many teachers are great at "just knowing" how their students are doing, few can articulate the research or pedagogy that backs up instructional best practices. This comes as no surprise. Since textbooks have traditionally done this work for us, there is little reason for teachers to understand the methodology of the instruction.

Marlena

In my early career, I was handed classroom after classroom with no curriculum, no textbooks, and an empty space. Through trial and error (and there were plenty of errors), I learned about instructional design theories as I created lessons from scratch that were interesting and engaging for my students.

We know that knowledge is power when it comes to translating practice into results in the classroom. A 2002 Stanford study found that teachers who were prepared to teach were more effective in supporting student achievement than teachers who did not participate in a preparation program or were not certified. Now that you are designing instruction or considering the implementation of EduProtocols in the classroom, school, or district, it is valuable to brush up on learning theories and to be able to validate and substantiate what appears to be a different approach to teaching when parents and administrators ask about it. And you can rest assured knowing the theories that back the EduProtocols are not new!

In this chapter, we will discuss some of the learning theories behind EduProtocols and show how they connect and support the EduProtocols (though there are many more theories than we will be able to cover here). The learning theories we focus on developed over time as educational theorists built upon the research that came before, so many of the theories overlap.

We provide here a simplified version of a few theories. This chapter is not intended to cover all the theories or the highly detailed components of each theory, but we think it will help you understand how long-established and researched instructional design theories relate to and support EduProtocols.

Lesson Design Theory

There are many learning theories and learning philosophies we can leverage not only to understand why our lessons work or don't work but also to guide us in how we design our lessons.

Three main instructional design domains.

- **Cognitivism**: How we think and process. This theory focuses on the learner and how they remember and understand information.
- **Constructivism**: How students construct knowledge. This theory is grounded in the belief that students develop their understanding of the world based on their experiences.
- **Behaviorism**: Building habits based on stimulus. Behaviorism theories are based on positive and negative interactions and how those influence behavior and habits.

Using the SPIRIT best practices for EduProtocols (covered earlier in the book), we can explore the claims of the EduProtocols and see how they measure up.

The six SPIRIT tips for successfully implementing the EduProtocols in the classroom are . . .

- **S**erious Commitment
- **P**rogression
- **I**mmediate Feedback
- **R**eps
- **I**nterest
- **T**ech Balance

S&P Claim 1: Serious Commitment

Use the protocol weekly, all semester, or all year long so students gain fluency with the process, which will enable them to focus on the content.

Claim 2: Progression

The first two reps of a protocol should focus on a non-academic, low-cognitive-load task so students can concentrate on the task, not the content. Educators should focus on students completing the protocol—quality may be low at first.

Theory: Cognitive Load Theory

The Cognitive Load Theory connects to the first two SPIRIT points: Seriously Committed and Progression.

Marlena sat in the passenger seat of the car one afternoon clutching the door handle while her new teen was in the driver's seat with a smile from ear to ear. She pulled out of the parking spot, crept to the exit, looked both ways, and proceeded to pull into the street, never once seeing the pedestrian crossing in front of them. A new driver is overloaded by the processes of driving, navigating, watching out for people and cars, and generally moving from point A to point B. All that processing takes a lot of brain power! Due to the potentially dangerous learning curve, the adult in the car helps the new learner manage this overload until the process of driving becomes second nature for the new learner. Teachers should handle the implementation of EduProtocols in precisely the same way.

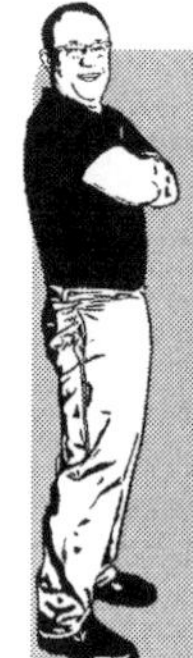

Jon

Gradual release is different from I do, we do, you do. It is cycling through an easier version and then scaling up in difficulty as students reach mastery.

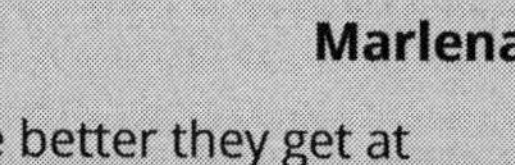

Marlena

The better they get at something, the harder we make it! That is where rigor is developed.

John Sweller developed the Cognitive Load Theory in 1988 and published it in the journal *Cognitive Science*. The Cognitive Load Theory (CLT) is an instructional design theory that explains how we process new information. According to CLT, new information processes in the working memory, and the mind can only handle a limited amount of incoming information in this space at one time. Too much incoming information makes our mind process too fast, and eventually the working memory shuts down.

New information is cycled through the short-term memory until it's processed long enough that it can move into the long-term memory. Once this information is in the long-term memory, new information can be added to expand this understanding. As concepts become more complicated, the understanding grows, and the brain can handle the burden of even more complicated input, whereas this was not possible at the outset.

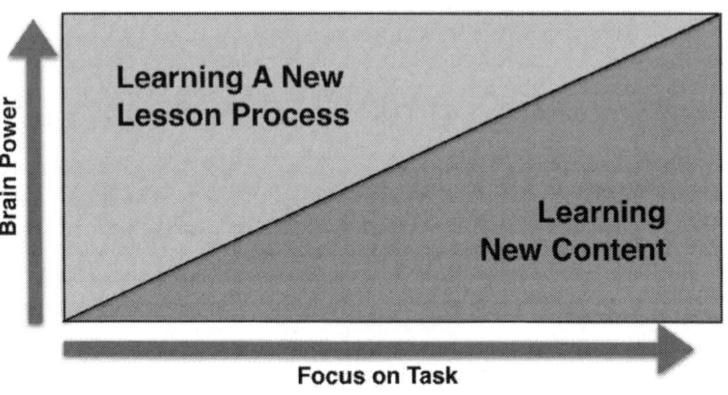

How to Apply Cognitive Load Theory to EduProtocols

When we ask students to process both a new lesson model and new content, the working memory cannot keep up. Students must focus on one part at a time until the process moves to the long-term memory and becomes second nature. Only then can a learner focus on new content. So use caution when adding new EduProtocols to the class routine—go slow to go fast! Use low-cognitive-load content in the first couple of reps so the students can focus on the model. As the model process becomes an afterthought, the content can become more rigorous. Commit to using the protocol regularly so students can move past the cognitive overload. Keep in mind that the theory applies not only to the learning of a protocol but also to the mastering of new subject matter content.

Go Slow to Go Fast Growth

We slow down until we "get" it.

Mastery and efficiency

Using the old feels easy

Learning something new is messy

Momentum builds as it becomes familiar

Claim 3: Immediate Feedback

Develop for immediate feedback. Get immediate impact.

Theory: Mastery Learning

Edward Thorndike, a behaviorist researcher of the early 1900s, experimented to see if repetition without feedback would result in learning. It did not. His subjects made absolutely no progress whatsoever. Participants just kept guessing for days, since they did not know if they were right or wrong. From Thorndike's 1932 Law of Exercises theory, we know that repetition without feedback does not result in much of anything productive. Using this new information, the concept of mastery learning was later developed by Morrison in the 1930s and was developed further by Benjamin Bloom in the 50s and 60s. The resulting theory assumes that all students can learn to a level of mastery and that by providing feedback midway through the process, subjects are provided opportunities to master the content. Today we refer to this as formative assessment: teach, assess, feedback, re-teach, and test.

Marlena

You likely remember Benjamin Bloom's Taxonomy of the hierarchy of learning from your teacher preparation classes.

Jon

Nothing is better than TWA (Teaching while Walking Around) in action!

How to Apply the Mastery Learning Theory to EduProtocols

Instead of teaching from the front of the room in a lecture-style classroom, EduProtocols free the teacher to provide individuals and groups of students immediate and ongoing feedback *during* the learning cycle.

If you are using tools such as Google Apps, feedback can also be quickly written, in real time, right on the student's paper as the teacher checks on student progress. With EduProtocols in which students are presenting their findings, feedback can be given immediately following the presentation. In general, kids need to know how they are doing, and the sooner they know, the faster they can implement the feedback provided to them. This shortened feedback loop will assist in accelerating the learning cycle as we increase both the opportunities for feedback and the time between when the students receive feedback and implement action(s) in response.

R Claim 4: Reps

We can't do a million reps in class, but we can do twenty or thirty (or more).

Theory: Elaboration Theory

The Elaboration theory, based on constructivism, states that curriculum difficulty is scaled up through repetitions of the whole task, much like following a recipe! Remember that time you decided to use a new recipe for a very special occasion? Perhaps it was your mom's birthday, and you decided to make some of the lovely red velvet cupcakes you found on Pinterest. The only problem was, you had never made cupcakes before, much less red velvet cupcakes.

You found yourself presented with two options:

- Mix one ingredient at a time and wait until next year to add the next ingredient after you had finally mastered mixing the first two. (Isn't this how we present many subjects to kids?)
- Take on a little cake batter and icing and go for the whole thing at once.

You worked all afternoon, and while the cupcakes left much to be desired, it was ok because mom would think you nailed it!

Pinterest cupcake

My cupcake: nailed it!

The next month was Dad's birthday, and you decided to give it another go. This time you avoided some of the pitfalls from attempt number one, and the cupcakes turned out a little better. In a few weeks, you decided to try again, and this time they actually looked like cupcakes. As in the Elaboration theory, you developed skill after repeating all the steps of the same or a similar task. You would have never presented your mom with a half-completed cupcake!

Marlena

"Hey mom, here is your flour and baking powder. Next year I'm going to add the sugar!"

How to Apply the Elaboration Theory to EduProtocols

As in Cyber Sandwich, the task is presented in its whole form right from the start. Students may not be proficient in their ability to complete the task yet, but as they practice, they *will* develop proficiency.

Marlena

8pARTs, Worst Preso Ever, and the Iron Chef (from *The EduProtocol Field Guide, Book One*) are all excellent examples of EduProtocols that develop proficiency through the application of the Elaboration theory.

Jon

The first attempts will be wonky at best (sometimes they are horrific), but they will get better with each rep. Keep the timeframes short to limit the feeling of failure!

Marlena

This is the point at which you embellish the protocols to enhance the rigor to meet your state standards by layering on your expectations for performance.

As students progress through the process, the project task becomes a little more polished and a little easier to accomplish. Students are building a conceptual schema and then strengthening and deepening the schema over time. The elements are the same, but the project becomes more complex as contents are deepened. Elaboration theory claims that students build upon prior learnings to scale up to the knowledge and understanding they need through the practice of the whole, and EduProtocols are structured just this way! Most protocols present students with the whole task the very first time. They learn the protocol by doing the protocol. They learn the curriculum by engaging with the curriculum. The task becomes more complicated and polished with each repetition, and students become ready for more complexity.

I Claim 5: Interest:

Just the right amount of content for the right amount of time.

Theory: Zone of Proximal Development

The Zone of Proximal Development is part of the Constructivism theory, where students work within a difficulty range that is not too hard or too easy. We have all had a student with a hoodie pulled over their head at least once in our careers, and we know that when that happens, no good will come of it! Our goal as teachers is to increase assimilation of knowledge while eliminating shutdown due to boredom or overload. The tricky part is finding just the right level and amount of content for each learner.

When students are allowed to construct their understanding of content, they tend to work at the level that allows them to learn the most. In other words, students will find a challenge that is within their reach if they are supported and given the opportunity and options to do so.

How to Apply the Zone of Proximal Development Theory to EduProtocols

Jon often says that the first attempts will be "super sucky," but with practice, they will get better. We foster this kind of improvement when we place students on a sliding scale of difficulty versus length of activity and provide enough structure to the learning to allow students to work within their Zone of Proximal Development. Then we provide enough flexibility and support to be sure students end up working where they best fit.

The result is that there will be a range of outcomes, but students will be working within their Zone of Proximal Development to minimize frustration and maximize learning.

Here are a few additional support structures that teachers can place within the structure of the protocol to support different learners (we will cover more in the next chapter on Universal Design for Learning):

- Pre-reading content before using the protocol
- Providing reading material at different levels of difficulty so students can choose
- Scaffolding with video before reading (use closed captions and translation in YouTube for English Language Learners)
- Allowing speech-to-text to minimize typing
- Allowing students to create images to illustrate understandings

Marlena

A common mistake teachers make when deploying EduProtocols is creating a long and detailed assignment within the protocol format and then giving students a ten-minute work period when they should have broken the assignment into two or more sections.

Jon

Cannot stress this enough! Shorten up the assignment or segment using EduProtocol Stacking or Smashing. Allowing for shorter bursts of work will allow students to find their flow.

T Claim 6: Tech Balance

Sometimes paper is faster.

Cognitive Load Theory and Zone of Proximal Development

We know from our many years of combined experience that balance is essential for producing healthy kids. Sometimes paper is more fitting, and sometimes technology can facilitate a better out-

English Language Learner Tip: *When showing video, closed captions are especially helpful in supporting the language acquisition and reading skills of ELLs.*

Jon

When I used the above approaches at Minarets High School, it was amazing to see "levels" disappear in classes. Creativity and critical thinking rapidly replaced memorization as the vanguard in our classes. In a memorize-and-test environment, only a percentage of students will latch on to the content, resulting in a bell curve.

come. As all the theories are interrelated on a sliding scale of sorts, there is a tipping point where one tool outweighs the other.

How to Apply the Theories to EduProtocols:

Consider the Zone of Proximal Development and Cognitive Load theories as explained above when deciding about when to use or not use technology. We know that not using technology is no longer an option! If you are a teacher saying, "Kids need balance," but in your classroom the laptops only come out on Fun Friday, we hope you will take this book to heart and begin to change your practice wherever you are in K–12 education. Remember: Go slow to go fast!

Additional Theories to Support EduProtocols

Claim: Collaboration

Many of the EduProtocols are collaborative.

Theory: Social Constructivism

Consider the speed of communication using email on a desktop versus text messaging on a phone. In a few quick text messages, we can tell our spouse what to pick up at the store in real time as they are standing in the aisle scratching their head over the red chili sauce or the enchilada sauce.

The publication of *The Social Construction of Reality* by Berger and Luckman in 1966 began to build upon the idea that students learn from interacting with their peers in real time.

Social Constructivism is based on the idea that we learn best from our peers and from working in a situation where we can dialogue and debate *in real time*. Getting instant feedback from peers allows for rapid learning cycles.

Social Constructivism also claims that each student develops their understanding by creating or constructing their knowledge as they dialogue through challenges with their peers.

Support from peers allows for faster speed, and faster speed allows for a faster growth cycle. In the right environment, we can trust our students to give and receive the feedback they need to grow. This instantaneous learning cycle provides intense feedback that easily outpaces TWA alone. TWA used in conjunction with Social Constructivism can create a powerful combination of support, feedback, and collaboration.

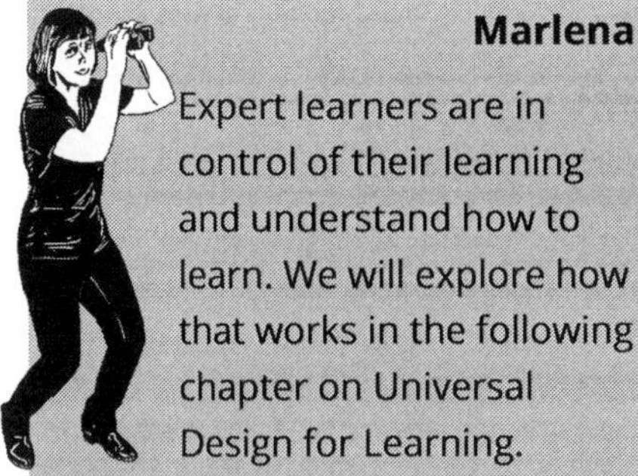

Marlena

Expert learners are in control of their learning and understand how to learn. We will explore how that works in the following chapter on Universal Design for Learning.

English Language Learner Tip: *Allowing ELLs to have purposeful engagement and meaningful interaction with peers is one of the most powerful ways to acquire the targeted language. Providing scaffolds for ELLs goes a long way.*

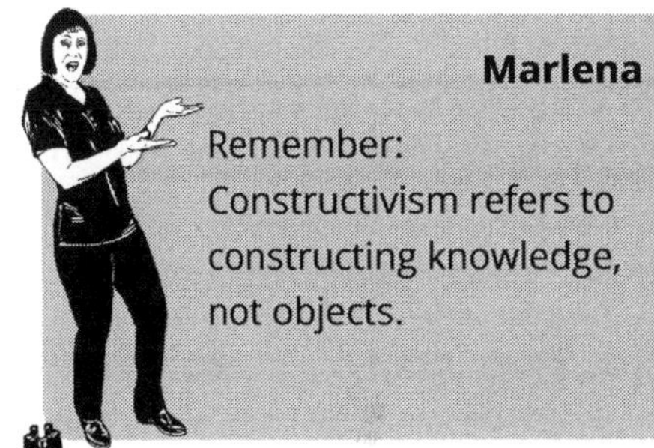

Marlena

Remember: Constructivism refers to constructing knowledge, not objects.

How to Apply the Social Constructivism Theory to EduProtocols

With many EduProtocols, students work collaboratively and in various student-centered groupings to develop their understanding of content. Peer-to-peer, real-time feedback speeds up the growth cycle as students ask for and receive help in finding answers to their questions as they arise. It also helps them construct new meanings and understandings as they experiment through trial and error and move through the curriculum. Encourage students to talk, to share, to explore as they work, and to be ready to explain to classroom visitors that this is how learning looks and sounds!

English Language Learner Tip: *Allow ELLs to take ownership of their learning by making content relevant and student centered. Students will put their heart and soul into learning when it is meaningful to them!*

Jon

Rarely are EduProtocols meant to be deployed in a quiet classroom! While there are quiet periods, much of the learning is animated and messy.

***English Language Learner Tip:** EduProtocols work for ALL ELLs. "I use these protocols in my Newcomers' classroom at least once a week." -Efraín Tovar*

***English Language Learner Tip:** EduProtocols allow ELLs to take ownership of their own learning.*

Marlena

Open the door and own it!

Call to Action

Become familiar with the claims of the EduProtocols and be prepared to explain learning theories to justify your instructional methods when parents or other educators ask!

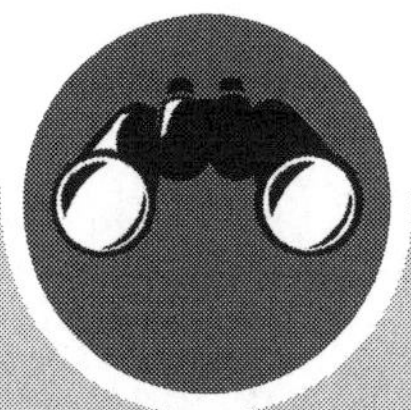

Chapter 25
Universal Design for Learning

You never really understand a person until you consider things from his point of view . . . Until you climb inside of his skin and walk around in it.

—Harper Lee, *To Kill a Mockingbird*

Universal Design for Learning

"Janell, what happened to your glasses?" Mrs. Garcia asked.

"Ummm, my sister broke 'em."

Recognizing the need to help Janell as best she could for today's lesson, Mrs. Garcia asked her, "Do you remember how to zoom in on the text on your Chromebook so you can see the text more clearly?"

"Yes, I do," Janell exclaimed as she turned her Chromebook for her teacher to view. "See?"

"Good. But listen here, *Mijita*," Mrs. Garcia affectionately chided Janell, "You still need to bring your glasses tomorrow!"

Marlena

A good teacher would never knowingly leave a student in the back of the room who is unable to see what is happening on the board. The barrier of text size is removed by thoughtful teachers all the time!

Mrs. Garcia helping Janell remove the barrier of text size is an example of Universal Design for Learning (UDL) in its simplest form. In its more complex form, educators will seek to remove a variety of learning barriers from students in need and then make those options open to all learners. Learners are then guided to reflect upon their work and project feedback for the effectiveness of their chosen options so they can make better choices next time.

The goal of UDL is to develop self-directed learners who can use their understanding of how they best learn to make decisions for engaging with and processing content.

A Very Short Guide to UDL

According to the Center for Applied Special Technology (CAST), the original designers of Universal Design for Learning, there are three basic elements to UDL:

1. Factors that motivate students to learn about a particular topic
2. How information goes in and is processed in the mind
3. How the student will demonstrate an understanding of the material covered

These three processes are referred to as . . .

Engagement	*How a student relates their personal "why" to an activity.* *What is their motivation to engage?*
Representation	*How a learner constructs an understanding of what they see, hear, and read.*
Action and Expression	*How a learner expresses their understanding gained in the Representation phase.*

Educators can *support the learning process* for students in each of the three areas.

Engagement	***Foster Engagement by offering topics that are irresistible to the learner and allowing choice in topics and/or aspects of study.***
Representation	***Foster Representation by providing options and allowing choices for how to engage with the content to be learned.***
Action and Expression	***Foster Action and Expression by giving students choice in the demonstration of skills or understandings.***

Developing Self-Directed Learners

Jon

Remember: Feedback should be ongoing, not just at the end of the lesson. Remember to use TWA!

If the end goal of UDL is to develop self-directed learners, then the last and most crucial part of UDL is for learners to reflect upon the choices they have made. When the work or project is completed and the instructor gives final feedback (with or without a grade), the student will spend a little time in reflection.

With work and teacher feedback in hand, students should be guided to ask themselves questions such as these:

- Was the choice I made (in this lesson or unit) the best one for me?
- How did I learn my best by making that choice?
- What can I do next time to make better choices and to be a better learner?

Teachers should ask themselves the following questions:

- What barriers do students face that continue to keep them from fully engaging with the content?
- How might I provide additional or different options that will remove any remaining barriers for specific students?
- How can I make those options available to everyone?

UDL Friendly

We say that EduProtocols are "UDL friendly," but what does this mean? If I take an EduProtocol off the shelf, will it meet the UDL requirements of my district?

Unfortunately, it isn't an easy question to answer, since UDL in your classroom will reflect adaptations that are specific to the learners in your environment. But being "UDL friendly" does mean that each EduProtocol contains some built-in flexibility as-is, "off the shelf," and most EduProtocols can easily be further adapted to incorporate multiple-media options to remove barriers for learning differences.

As an example, let's analyze the EduProtocol Sketch and Tell and focus on Representation to explore how UDL might fit in this EduProtocol model and how we might adjust the protocol to meet the needs of particular students in our class more effectively.

In Sketch and Tell, students read a passage and then create a graphic representation or model of what they understand or of the concepts in the reading material. They share the graphic representation with a partner then follow it with a brief written paragraph to explain and summarize their learning of that concept.

As we have structured it, Sketch and Tell utilizes reading, comprehension, interpretation and modeling, and writing. If provided with appropriately leveled reading passages, students will read and write at their particular academic levels. That written content could be provided in different formats for students who still struggle to comprehend the written content.

A video with subtitles, an audio recording, or text-to-speech automated reading would enable students who struggle to read at their grade level to digest the necessary concepts and achieve the goals for the lesson. One modification like this might make all the difference for students in your class!

Marlena

Think of EduProtocols like one of our favorite and most engaging games, Othello: They take a minute to learn and a lifetime to master! Use EduProtocols "off the shelf," and as you become more proficient teaching with them, you'll find creative ways to adapt them to fit your learners.

Student Cases

We are going to explore how the EduProtocol Sketch and Tell can be modified to meet the needs of two students. As we analyze these two student cases, consider how the tips mentioned here can also be used to benefit other learners in your class.

The first student is Samantha, whose specific learning challenges, strengths, and weaknesses are documented in her SPED profile. The second student is Brady, who is working slightly above grade level. Through the process of analyzing Samantha's known modifications and Brady's needs as a learner, we will begin to develop an understanding of how barriers affect and can be removed for a wide range of learners regardless of their status as SPED, mainstream, English learners, or general education. We will then explore how these recommendations are inherently present or may be easily added to enhance the UDL qualities of many EduProtocols.

Student One Profile: Samantha

Samantha is a young fifth-grade student. She is reading about two levels below her grade. She is an eager student, but she shuts down easily when the material is too difficult for her. Samantha has difficulty accessing grade-level curriculum independently in all content areas. (Sound familiar?) Her challenges carry over to math, as she isn't able to comprehend the grade-level word problems well enough to solve them on her own. Samantha has difficulty in the area of writing (in conventions and structure). When CAASSP testing (California's statewide testing), she will not be allowed to have accommodation/modification because she isn't far enough behind to qualify for them. (We have many students that fall into this gray area. Only one percent of the student population per test may receive accommodations or modifications on state testing in California.)

Jon

Removing barriers isn't a SPED issue! All learners have barriers to learning that need to be considered, and it's our job to help remove these barriers every day, in every lesson.

Accommodations

If we take all the accommodations outlined in Samantha's IEP and sort them according to the three areas of Universal Design

Jon

Sometimes a boring lesson is simply a boring lesson, and only *certain students* will *willingly* engage with a boring process. Try something new when that happens—provide options, or direct topics and lessons to students' interests.

for Learning—Engagement, Representation, and Action and Expression—we can create a plan for each area like those explained below. (This is where we practice removing barriers!)

Engagement

Learning begins with a student's desire to engage in a learning experience. Understanding Samantha's motivation for participation will dictate the way Samantha dials into this lesson.

Offering student-centered lessons in which students construct their learning will allow Samantha wiggle room in finding her purpose. Couple that with fun, high-energy, supportive teammates with whom to work, exciting prompts, and supportive feedback, and our students may find deeper motivation by being part of the process. Students find motivation in different aspects of life and work: advocacy, informative, experimental, artistry, or in the collaboration itself. One of these may work for Samantha.

The more we can connect the content to the things our students are passionate about, the more easily we can win this one. Remember: The ability to choose direction, subtopics, or method of engagement is also an empowering option for students.

Representation

The identified Representation accommodations that are to be considered for Samantha include the following:

- Visual presentations paired with repeated oral explanations
- Digital audio/cd content
- Visual organizer/graphic organizer
- Text-to-speech
- Books on tape
- Pair with a peer for reading support during class
- Separate spelling program from the curriculum
- Options for appropriate ability-leveled books rather than grade-level books to meet grade-level standards

Marlena

There is more than one way to present the content to Samantha. We could also enable text-to-speech so Samantha could follow along with the same passage the rest of the class is reading.

We know Samantha will have a difficult time reading the passage, so how might we structure Sketch and Tell to provide support for this one student? One way would be to embed a video before the reading passage to provide a scaffold for the reading or to serve as a replacement for the reading passage. This video would contain similar vocabulary and/or content to the written passage.

Now our student will be able to watch the video, hear the pronunciation of the words she is reading, and gain a sense of the concepts presented in the passage. And if we make sure the captions are turned on while she watches the video, we can reinforce the auditory connection to the written words as well. Once she finishes watching the video and/or reading the passage, she will be able to move on to Action and Expression and share what she has learned.

Marlena

This is big! That one simple gesture of allowing any student the option to use headphones to watch the same video provides Samantha with confidence and assurance that she fits in with her peers.

This example illustrates why Universal Design for Learning is such a powerful tool in the classroom. We have targeted this lesson to one specific struggling student, but in fact, the video we have provided may help other students as well, even those we consider to be our most successful learners. In the spirit of Universal Design for Learning, we will make this one accommodation an option for every student regardless of perceived ability. And by making the video a *choice for everyone*, we have empowered Samantha to feel normal when she puts on her headphones and watches the video because she no longer stands out as different from the other students in the class.

Jon

Helping Samantha feel "normal" makes learning in her class that much more fun and welcoming.

Other options for Samantha may include having the teacher read the passage aloud in a screencast while tracking the text. Another option might be to modify the passage to reduce the reading level for Samantha, making it more accessible for her reading level while maintaining the same content. And we would again make these options available to everyone in the class.

English Language Learner Tip: *Adding a language objective to your EduProtocol allows ELLs to know what is expected from them when expressing what they have learned.*

Action and Expression

While Representation is how students receive and process content, Action and Expression is how students show what they have learned. To align with the UDL model, students are provided choices in how they show their understanding of the content. We can adapt EduProtocols to accommodate choices in Action and Expression by building in response options for students. We have also structured Sketch and Tell so students create a graphic im-

Marlena

It is important to know what your learning objectives are. If your objective is to write a five-paragraph paper with well-developed introductory and concluding paragraphs, then allowing students to create a video is not a reasonable option. Perhaps speech-to-text is more fitting.

Jon

The options you offer must be aligned with the learning objectives.

age of their understanding, explain their drawing to a partner, and write a short paragraph explaining what they know.

The IEP recommendations for Samantha's Action and Expressions accommodation are as follows:

- Speech-to-text (so she can create written work faster)
- Screencast oral responses
- Oral responses
- Recorded responses

We know Samantha struggles with the barrier of writing. The first two items on Samantha's Action and Expression list address this barrier: speech-to-text and screencast oral responses. We can allow Samantha the choice of one or more of these adaptations, giving her the opportunity to share, unhindered, the full extent of her knowledge with us.

Meanwhile, back at Sketch and Tell . . .

If you remember, there are three parts to the Sketch and Tell EduProtocol:

- Read a passage and then create a graphic representation or model of the concepts presented.
- Share it with a partner.
- Write a brief paragraph to explain and summarize their knowledge.

In part one, "Read a passage," we can use a video, recording of the passage, or text-to-speech to help Samantha read the passage. Then Samantha will draw a visual representation of the reading. We expect that Samantha would be just fine doing this part without a modification, since drawing is not included in her list of barriers.

We also expect Samantha to do reasonably well with part two, "Share with a partner," since this is an oral discussion. Samantha is shy, so you might have to consider how to pair her with the right partner in the beginning.

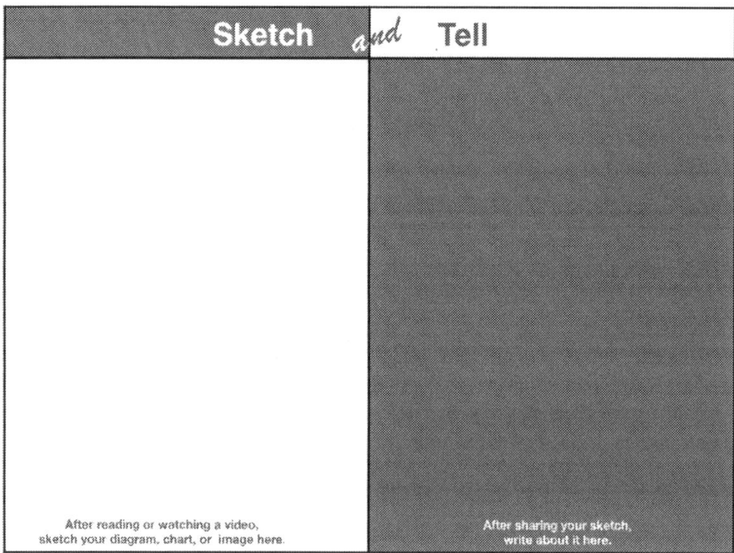

Sketch and Tell
After reading or watching a video, sketch your diagram, chart, or image here.
After sharing your sketch, write about it here.

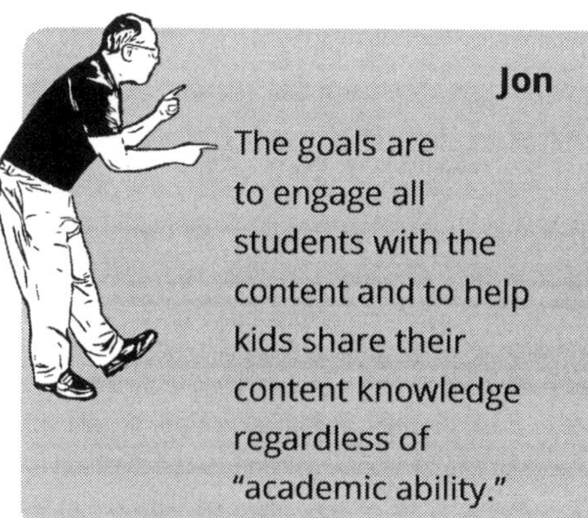

Jon
The goals are to engage all students with the content and to help kids share their content knowledge regardless of "academic ability."

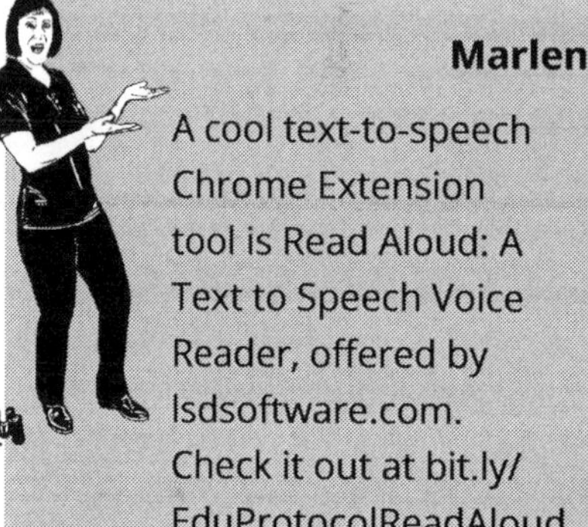

Marlena
A cool text-to-speech Chrome Extension tool is Read Aloud: A Text to Speech Voice Reader, offered by lsdsoftware.com. Check it out at bit.ly/EduProtocolReadAloud.

Part three of Sketch and Tell is to write a brief paragraph. Samantha will become more invested in the learning experience as we reduce or remove certain barriers for her. One way to do that is to replace the written paragraph with a recording of Samantha talking about what she learned. Another way is by using a secondary program such as Flipgrid to record a response. Lastly, Samantha could use a text-to-speech option within her word processing program to assist her in her writing. The goal of the Sketch and Tell activity is to help students understand the content at a deeper level, so all these replacement options would still allow Samantha to meet the curricular goal. And of course, in the spirit of UDL, we will make that accommodation available to all students.

Marlena

Sometimes we link quick little video tutorials into student work or a resource page, and Samantha would do well with the visual and auditory nature of video help tutorials.

Feedback

When providing the final feedback for Sketch and Tell, Samantha's teacher will consider all the options presented, such as speech-to-text, text-to-speech, screencasting, etc. Remember that even though the options were provided for Samantha, she may choose not to use them. Samantha will reflect on her choices, and we must respect her decision in making them.

Student Two Profile: Brady

The second student is Brady. Brady is outgoing and a little more confident than Samantha in his abilities. He is reading above grade level. He is bright and quick and gets bored easily when his peers work slowly. The biggest challenge his teacher faces is keeping Brady moving forward in reading instruction while also supporting grade-level content standards. As you read through this section, think about how some of the barriers we removed for Samantha may affect Brady as well.

Jon

The available tools and options may change depending on the lesson objectives.

Accommodations

Brady does not have formal accommodations. Ideally, his teachers will try to keep him challenged and working at his reading level but with the same content instruction as the rest of the class instead of moving him into an independent work model. Engaging Brady's higher reading level while opening opportunities for Brady to collaborate and work with his peers will help him to continue to develop the essential Four Cs (collaboration, critical thinking, communication, and creativity) and "soft" skills.

Jon

Remember: As we make new elements available to all learners, they may choose not to use them!

Engagement

Engaging Brady initially is fairly easy, but maintaining engagement can be challenging. Brady likes to feel that his work has a purpose. He is quick to reject work that he views as "busy work" and replaces it with goofing around. Providing irresistible topics and projects will capture the attention of even the most reluctant learner, and this autonomy is an important aspect of a UDL classroom.

Marlena

Learners will need time to reflect on what worked best for them so they can make better choices next time.

Representation

Representation is how information is processed and makes sense to the learner. Allowing options for engaging with the content enables Brady to feel comfortable diving into more difficult reading, especially when he can use the supporting videos to help ensure he is comprehending the content. Brady feels the videos are interesting and help him to understand, and it's okay for him to use them, as these are options presented to the whole class in our UDL adaptation of Sketch and Tell.

Action and Expression

Action and Expression are how students show what they have learned. Brady's teacher purposefully builds in options for Action and Expression that she knows Brady will enjoy, such as making a screencast or using image search to enhance presentations. Even through Brady does not seem like an overly creative student, showing what he knows in an original way is what engages Brady the most, and he often goes above and beyond what is required when he finds the work fun.

Self-Directed Learners

To complete the UDL cycle of learning, allow students to take a few minutes to reflect on the choices they've made and the effect those choices have had on their learning. Students should use their project, grade, and feedback from their teacher and/or peers as support for their conclusions.

If, for example, a student who has difficulty processing oral material watched the video because it was faster but did not understand the concepts presented, he may not have engaged with the curriculum in the best way for him. Or perhaps a student discovers they had a difficult time reading the written material in the time allowed but were able to skim the written material after watching the video. Using a combination of video and text might have been a better option for that student.

Our higher calling as teachers is to help each student become a lifelong learner. To do that, we must help students understand how they learn best.

Jon

We adults are aware of and often think about how we learn best. Our lifetime of trial and error has taught us well. We must help students achieve the same awareness before they leave us.

Marlena

It is impossible to know all the barriers each student faces. I once had a student an entire year before the parents disclosed that he had had a brain tumor removed as a toddler.

UDL-ify EduProtocols

What are some options for removing barriers for students as they use EduProtocols? Below are some tips and suggestions you might consider while planning. Also consider other options that are available in your district. This list can be overwhelming, and we are not suggesting that you tackle it all at once. Start with your most needy student and make the options available to everyone.

Engagement

- EduProtocols are high in engagement due to the fun factor we try to build into each activity. Lowering the cognitive load by using an EduProtocol over and over (reps) allows most students to get past the technology barriers of working online and get into the content. High-performing teachers establish and maintain a fun environment while also assisting students who are having difficulty with technology. We understand that fun may not resonate with every student, so adjust the tempo as needed.
- One key practice for EduProtocols is timing activities so students sustain a higher level of concentration for shorter periods of time. You know your students best, of course, and you know for whom this strategy may be problematic. Adjust and modify for that learner as needed (perhaps by simplifying a reading selection).
- Increase the relevance and engagement factor by using topics that are of high interest to your particular students or adjust the EduProtocol so that it relates to ongoing classroom projects that are already high in student agency.

English Language Learner Tip: *Allowing ELLs to collaborate by using their primary language (L1) with other ELLs is a powerful way to engage students while acknowledging their identity. Language is tied to identity!*

English Language Learner Tip: *Wait time is especially important for ELLs. It gives them time to think and formulate what they want to say in a language that is still becoming second nature.*

Representation

1. Structure processing time for students.
2. Use various methods to remove barriers:
    a. Short videos to support main concepts
    b Vocabulary support
        i. Link to a page or a teacher-created screencast that explains a word.
        ii. Link to a YouTube video that pronounces the word right in the text.
    c. Screencast of you reading the passage aloud so students can follow along (Open the passage on your computer

and read it so the recording contains both the written material and your voice reading it aloud.)

d. Visuals such as diagrams and charts to reinforce the content

3. Be sure to make all the options you add available to all students.

Action and Expression

1. Keep in mind your goal for the activity. If the goal is for students to write a five-paragraph essay, students will need to write an essay. (Keep in mind the IEP, if in place, as a guide for how to modify a particular assignment.) If your goal is for students to understand and explain the American westward expansion, then allow alternate options for doing so.
2. Build in more than one method to evaluate student understanding.
3. Use these methods to remove barriers:
   a. Screencasts/videos
   b. Text-to-speech
   c. Digital sketchnoting or diagrams
4. Allow students choice in how they show what they know.

English Language Learner Tip: *Using translation apps and/or websites (e.g., Google Translate, WordReference, WordSift, ReWordify) to give access to key vocabulary words is invaluable. Help students learn to use these resources on their own so they can access them when needed.*

Implementation of UDL Elements

When implementing these UDL elements, think about how students will use them. Some, like using video for Representation, have fairly natural implementation flows. Just click and watch, right?

It might be helpful, however, to consider how students are watching the video. Do they have access? Do they need to get up and go across the room to get their headphones? Is that a disruption to others? How will this activity flow in your class?

How about something a little harder, like making a screencast as a video response? Allow students time to create and experiment with a first screencast in a low-cognitive-load environment before the assignment is given. Once the assignment goes live, you will

English Language Learner Tip: *Want to learn more about UDL and English Language Learners? For more information, visit Language Magazine's article, "Why UDL Matters for English Language Learners" with Katie Novak at bit.ly/EduProtocol-ELL-TIPS.*

Marlena

Sometimes you have to walk a thin line to balance the proficiency of the group with the ability to move forward with the task.

want the lesson flow to be as smooth as possible with as few disruptions as possible.

What considerations will you need to make? Do students need training in the classroom processes? Set students up for success ahead of time!

Adding UDL

Follow this process to add additional UDL elements to your EduProtocols:

1. Train your students on the EduProtocol without modifications. Make sure they understand the basic flow.
2. Allow practice time for all students in a separate session on the UDL element you wish to add.
3. Once the basic EduProtocol is mastered and the new element is also introduced, give students the choice to combine them into one.
4. When introducing a new EduProtocol, make sure students are up to speed on the new protocol before adding additional UDL elements, as this complicates the basic structure of the EduProtocol. (There may be exceptions for when to add an additional element, so use your awesome teacher judgment.)
5. Since we want students to make informed choices, be sure the group of students most in need of the options is also most familiar with the options. Allow for additional practice prior to the lesson or solicit the assistance of SPED or push-in aides.

Call to Action

Identify one student in your class and plan to implement one or more tools that will remove the barriers for that student when deploying an EduProtocol.

Reflect with students about how they learned best after you have implemented the EduProtocol. Your goal here is to help them become self-directed learners. Pay particular attention to your one student. Did the element you added support this student? If not, does this student need more practice with that particular element or a different one entirely? Adjust the lesson for next time as needed.

Did other students take advantage of the element you added? How did the added element support other learners in your class?

Need more? Check out the resources and research on cast.org for more information to support UDL, theories of learning, and best practices for teachers.

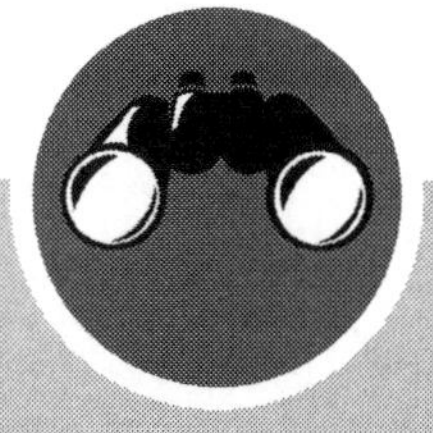

Chapter 26
School-Wide EduProtocol Implementation

It is time to make a priority of inspiring lives over following teacher editions.

—Marlena Hebern

Whether you are a superintendent implementing EduProtocols across your district, a principal implementing EduProtocols in your school, or a coach implementing EduProtocols in a few classrooms, there are some tips and tricks we want to share with you that we have learned along the way from our experiences working with districts.

The first thing to remember in planning for implementing EduProtocols is that no matter how hard you try, not everyone is going to be on board. Erika Anderson, a founding partner of Proteus, points out in her blog post "The Secret to Getting Really, Really Good at Something" that, "Getting good at something means going through various periods of being not-good, during which you tend to feel dumb, clueless, incompetent. Many people would simply rather not go through that." Anderson also points out that "lack of belief in oneself is by far the greatest impediment to success." It is essential that districts allow a safe space for teachers to develop mastery. Teachers who might hold back on the initial implementation effort will join in when they believe it is safe enough to try.

An effective approach that we have seen for implementing a change in the school setting is to begin on a "test pilot" model. Start with a core of teachers that are excited about the topic and build momentum from there.

Kimberly Vogue uses youcubed.org to assist in implementation. Teachers select one of 25 books and a subscription box and materials are delivered in a couple of weeks. The teacher receives a HyperDoc, informative slide deck, and materials to assist them as they read the book. Additionally, there are two face-to-face collaboration times where teachers from across the district meet to discuss the signature practices that support district-wide initiatives.

From Kimberly: *"The YOU Cube itself is a protocol. For me, as the creator of professional learning opportunities, I can easily replicate this model. Harnessing the power of the EduProtocol model allows me to ensure quality and streamlines planning and prep time. Time that I can spend researching best practices and modeling lessons in classrooms to support student-centered learning."*

Here's a checklist to get you started:

- Identify "signature practices"
- Select book titles
- Create a HyperDoc to accompany the book
- Locate "posters" or flyers to send
- Find swag to make it fun! (stickers, magnets, stationery)
- Communicate the offerings via a website with a place to order

Moore's Law of Diffusion states that the more someone sees something, the better chance they have of adopting it, and this "learning curve" applies to an organization as much as it does to an individual. We can use this wave of increasing potential in our implementation strategy when we allow teachers to come aboard in their own time. Once we reach about 16 percent implementation, Maloney's 16 Percent rule kicks in, which suggests that we are now positioned to see our message reach more than just the early adopters, as it begins to gain a greater general social acceptance. Maloney's 16 Percent rule also says that the upper group (the 16 percent) needs a different approach (much more edgy) than the other 84 percent. The lower 84 percent was skeptical, but after seeing some success, they were prepared to join in, provided the message presented the change as easy and normal. In a district setting, this growth in acceptance is accomplished through the sharing of best practices, peer PLCs, building and sharing resources, developing innovator groups, and/or creating a district-wide (or school-wide) community around the use of EduProtocols.

Two favorite EduProtocols for startup are The Fast and The Curious and Cyber Sandwich, first introduced in *The EduProtocol Field Guide, Book One.* The Fast and The Curious will help teachers recapture time in the classroom by teaching vocabulary and facts more quickly, thereby freeing up valuable instructional minutes for the protocol implementation. Cyber Sandwich is a versatile entry-level protocol that replaces the pair-share with an accountability model. It can easily be adapted to any annotation techniques teachers are already using while providing structured evidence of the pair-share.

Implement the Math Reps model by Lisa Nowakowski for mastery of math concepts in K–8 schools. Marlena also recommends implementing BookaKucha as a replacement for purchased library-reading assessment programs. An entire school can implement BookaKucha once a week for a snapshot of student reading and accountability, immediately freeing up resources for the continued implementation of EduProtocols.

Give yourself advantages at the middle and high school levels with just a few well-placed EduProtocols. For a teacher with five preps, the content changes from period to period, but by using an EduProtocol, the workflow stays the same. An English teacher can reuse the *same* EduProtocols by simply changing the book title for each class. Teachers "buy in" quickly when they realize they can create a manageable schedule while increasing student engagement and feedback.

Jon

The Fast and The Curious uses a quiz program to accelerate vocabulary instruction: test, feedback, test. Teachers are basically self-training on the potential of fast feedback, less lecture, and the lack of a need for tedious worksheets to collect and correct.

Detailed directions for The Fast and The Curious, Cyber Sandwich, Math Reps, and BookaKucha can all be found in The EduProtocol Field Guide, Book One.

As a New Textbook

Let's take a look at one southern California school district of about eight hundred teachers that just adopted new math textbooks. The new math books cost this district \$3.7 million. Nearly \$700,000, (20 percent) of the adoption was just shipping and handling. If we replace those books with OERs (open source educational materials), EduProtocols, and a few handpicked online materials, we can repurpose those dollars spent on shipping and invest them in teachers through professional development and unit planning. We can provide the resources needed for teachers to depart from the corporate textbook model. The remainder of the textbook purchasing cost can be used to replenish student devices.

Marlena

One central coast district helped teachers map textbooks to the standards, and when teachers realized they could do a better job of teaching standards and content, they willingly agreed to stop adopting their curriculum from publishers.

Some districts have worked out cost comparison models and shared them with teachers, so now it's common that conversations take place about curriculum and the investment in teachers vs. purchased programs. As a result of these conversations, some districts choose to implement EduProtocols with other resources instead of corporate textbooks, and others choose to use them as a supplement.

Jon

We've seen this implementation strategy work in district after district with initiative after initiative.

Working with Teachers

Shifting to a textbook-free environment is a difficult conversation to have with teacher groups who may not understand the change that is happening to instruction within their school. It is essential that the administration articulate that they are not just abandoning teachers and leaving them without a published curriculum. Our goal is to transition teachers to using EduProtocols and Open Educational Resources so they can experience the flexibility and empowerment of planning and writing customized curriculum. The beauty of the EduProtocols is that they can be modified to support classrooms and teachers all across this continuum of implementation and teacher skillset. And as schools begin to repurpose funds from textbooks to professional development, teachers will understand that they have the support they need to make this change, especially if they have hit Maloney's 16 percent implementation mark, and momentum is beginning to build.

Marlena

Assessment with EduProtocols couldn't be easier—students simply execute a protocol they *know* on content they may or may not have ever seen, and they do it by themselves.

EduProtocols as Assessment

EduProtocols make effective assessment systems, provided the district takes a few well-implemented EduProtocols and does a good job of designing and deploying them as assessments. Math reps can be used as an effective assessment system when the expectation is set that every student will achieve 100 percent mastery on the math rep of the week. The EduProtocols become the assessments for students. Iron Chef and Cyber Sandwich also make effective assessment tools. Students can design their own Iron Chefs or complete one that is presented to them. Cyber Sandwich is a wonderful structure to evaluate student reading and writing in response to a prompt.

English Language Learner Tip: *Use EduProtocols to seamlessly assess an ELL's language growth. Whether assessing the speaking, writing, and/or reading domains, the results will be shown in the end product.*

Call to Action

Think about what you need to do to share or implement EduProtocols where you are. Outline goals and actionable steps that you can take to begin using EduProtocols in your classroom, school, or district. At the district level, consider developing a customized scope and sequence of the EduProtocols that includes which ones will be implemented when and at which grade levels. Don't forget a training plan. Know how and when other teachers will receive training or classroom modeling of the protocols they are to implement. Then begin the process and set the wheels in motion! Be sure to share your success on Twitter using the hashtag #EduProtocols. And both Marlena and Jon are eager to help and advise. Reach out to us on Twitter: @jcorippo and @mhebern.

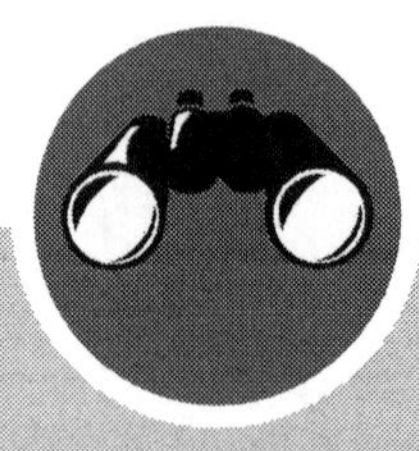

Thank You!

We have learned that writing a book takes a big team and a lot of time. And we want to thank those who have helped us along the way because we would never have completed a book without the following people!

Thank you to our spouses and families, especially Walt and Rhonda, for being so very understanding and supportive as we have worked late into the night writing and editing. Your love and support is a blessing!

Thank you, Dave and Shelley Burgess, for having faith in us and for saying yes to a second book! We love being a part of the DBC family!

Thank you, Erin Casey and the behind the scenes staff at My Writers' Connection, who worked their incredible magic to help us share our message and passion with educators!

You are amazing!

Thank you and a big shout out to the many teachers and educators who have tried EduProtocols, or shared their EduProtocols ideas with us! We love hearing what you are doing with kids! We are humbled by your honest and sincere engagement and willingness to try something new. You give us motivation, energy, and joy!

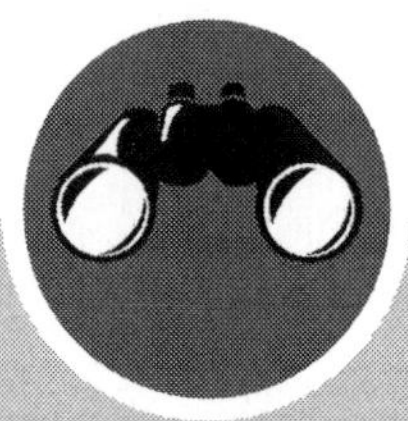

Notes

Preface

Viereck, George. "What Life Means to Einstein: An Interview by George Sylvester Viereck." *The Saturday Evening Post*, October 26, 1929.

Chapter 1

Rose, Todd, *End of Average: The Science of What Makes Us Different.* New York: HarperCollins, 2016.

Schoenberger, Karl. "Nintendo to Fund Learning Project at MIT." *LA Times* (Los Angeles, CA), May 16, 1990.

Knapton, Sarah. "Robots Will Take over Most Jobs within 30 Years, Experts Warn." *The Telegraph*, February 13, 2016. telegraph.co.uk/news/science/science-news/12155808/Robots-will-take-over-most-jobs-within-30-years-experts-warn.html.

Yan, Sophia. "Artificial Intelligence Will Replace Half of All Jobs in the Next Decade, Says Widely Followed Technologist." *CNBC*, April 27, 2017. cnbc.com/2017/04/27/kai-fu-lee-robots-will-replace-half-of-all-jobs.html.

Landes, David S. *The Unbound Prometheus: Technological Change and Industrial Development in Western Europe from 1750 to the Present*. Cambridge, New York: Press Syndicate of the University of Cambridge, 1969.

Horn, Jeff, Leonard Rosenband, and Merritt Roe Smith. *Reconceptualizing the Industrial Revolution*. Cambridge, MA: MIT Press, 2010.

Muntone, Stephanie. "Second Industrial Revolution." *Education.com*. The McGraw-Hill Companies. Archived from the original on 22 October 2013. Retrieved 14 October 2013.

Schoenherr, Steven E., (5 May 2004). "The Digital Revolution." Archived from the original on 7 October 2008.

Kim, Tae. "McDonald's Hits All-Time High as Wall Street Cheers Replacement of Cashiers with Kiosks." *CNBC*, June 22, 2017. cnbc.com/2017/06/20/mcdonalds-hits-all-time-high-as-wall-street-cheers-replacement-of-cashiers-with-kiosks.html.

Harbaugh, Jennifer. "Space Station 3-D Printer Builds Ratchet Wrench to Complete First Phase of Operations." *NASA*, December 22, 2014. nasa.gov/mission_pages/station/research/news/3Dratchet_wrench.

"The 5th Industrial Revolution: When It Will Happen and How." *DevOps.com*, December 24, 2017. devops.com/5th-industrial-revolution-will-happen/.

"Industrial Revolution." *History.com,* Accessed July 4, 2018. history.com/topics/industrial-revolution.

Yamei, "China Focus: AI Beats Human Doctors in Neuroimaging Recognition Contest." *XINHUANET,* June 30, 2018. xinhuanet.com/english/2018-06/30/c_137292451.htm.

"Concrete Product Machines and Solutions–Columbia Machine." *Columbia Machine*, Accessed June 4, 20148. columbiamachine.com.

Mahdawi, Arwa and Mona Chalabi. "What Jobs Will Still Be around in 20 Years? Read This to Prepare Your Future." *The Guardian,* June 26, 2017. theguardian.com/us-news/2017/jun/26/jobs-future-automation-robots-skills-creative-health.

Khan, Sal. "Let's Teach for Mastery—Not Test Scores." *TED.* Accessed April 3, 2019. ted.com/talks/sal_khan_let_s_teach_for_mastery_not_test_scores?language=en#t-2523.

"Moral Dilemmas for Japan's High-Tech Researchers." *The Japan Times*, April 9, 2018. japantimes.co.jp/opinion/2018/04/09/editorials/moral-dilemmas-japans-high-tech-researchers/#.XGnZbJP7QUt.

The Guardian. "The Last Job on Earth: Imagining a Fully Automated World." *YouTube.* February 17, 2016. youtube.com/watch?v=Yvs7f4UaKLo.

Johnson, David. "Find out If a Robot Will Take Your Job." *TIME*, April 19, 2017. time.com/4742543/robots-jobs-machines-work/.

Marzano, Robert, Debra Pickering, and Jane Pollock. *Classroom Instruction That Works: Research-Based Strategies for Increasing Student Achievement*. Boston, MA: Pearson Education, 2004.

Chapter 2

Calvo, Amanda. "J.K. Rowling Wishes Magic Could Get U.K. out of Brexit" *Time*, June 24, 2016.

Chapter 12

Gaffney, Dennis. "10 Surprising Civil War Facts." *History.* history.com/news/10-surprising-civil-war-facts. civilwar.org/learn/articles/civil-war-fact.

Chapter 18

Wiley, David. "What Is Open Pedagogy?" *OpenContent.org.* October 21, 2013. opencontent.org/blog/archives/2975.

Creative Commons. "About The Licenses." creativecommons.org/licenses/.

Attribution-ShareAlike: CC BY-SA: This license lets others remix, tweak, and build upon your work even for commercial purposes, as long as they credit you and license their new creations under the identical terms. This license is often compared to "copyleft" free and open source software licenses. All new works based on yours will carry the same license, so any derivatives will also allow commercial use. This is the license used by Wikipedia and is recommended for materials that would benefit from incorporating content from Wikipedia and similarly licensed projects.

Chapter 22

Grab, Michael. "Gravity Is the Only 'Glue' That Holds These Structures in Equilibrium." *Gravity Glue.* gravityglue.com/about/.

Sweller, John. "Cognitive Load during Problem Solving: Effects on Learning." *Cognitive Science*. April, 1988. onlinelibrary.wiley.com/doi/10.1207/s15516709cog1202_4.

Chapter 23

Bennetts, Leslie. "First Lady in Waiting." Quote from Michelle Obama's campaign speech: "I am desperate for change—now—not in 8 years or 12 years, but right now. We don't have time to wait." *Vanity Fair Online,* December, 2007.

Chapter 24

Darling-Hammond, Linda, Deborah Holtzman, Su Jin Gatlin, and Julian Vasquez Heilig. "Does Teacher Preparation Matter? Evidence about Teacher Certification, Teach for America, and Teacher Effectiveness." *Education Policy Analysis Archives.* Accessed July 14, 2018. epaa.asu.edu/ojs/article/view/147.

Schunk, Dale H. *Learning Theories: An Educational Perspective.* New York: Pearson, 2012.

"Learning Theories." *InstructionalDesign.org.* Accessed July 14, 2018. instructionaldesign.org/theories/.

"About Universal Design for Learning." *Cast.* Accessed July 17, 2018. cast.org/our-work/about-udl.html#.XGnhVJP7QUs.

Larson, Tony. "The 4Cs Research Series." BattelleforKids. p21.org/our-work/4cs-research-series. Accessed 22 Nov. 2018. [Links to new website, Batelle for Kids]

Alber, Rebecca. "6 Scaffolding Strategies to Use with Your Students." *edutopia*. May 24, 2011. edutopia.org/blog/scaffolding-lessons-six-strategies-rebecca-alber.

New Levine, Linda, Laura Lukens, and Betty Ansin Smallwood. "The GO TO Strategies: Scaffolding Options for Teachers of English Language Learners, K-12." *The University of Missouri-Kansas City and North Kansas City Schools.* Accessed December 19, 2018. ride.ri.gov/Portals/0/Uploads/Documents/Students-and-Families-Great-Schools/English-Language-Learners/go-to-strategies.pdf.

Houser, Kristin. "8 Strategies for Scaffolding Instruction." *Ms. Houser.* Accessed December 19, 2018. mshouser.com/teaching-tips/8-strategies-for-scaffolding-instruction.

Chapter 25

"About Universal Design for Learning." *Cast.* Accessed June 9, 2018. cast.org/our-work/about-udl.html#.XGnfJJP7QUs.

"Until Learning Has No Limits." CAST: About Universal Design for Learning, CAST, 22 June 2018, cast.org/, Accessed on 6/9/2018

Novak, Katie. "Why UDL Matters for English Language Learners." *Language Magazine*, March 9, 2018. languagemagazine.com/2018/03/09/why-udl-matters-for-english-language-learners/.

Chapter 26

When teachers rely on TE's, they teach for a day. When they design lessons, they inspire lives.– Marlena Hebern

"Diffusion of a Technology Usually Lags Performance." *Saylordotorg.* Accessed November 19, 2018. saylordotorg.github.io/text_developing-new-products-and-services/s04-08-diffusion-of-a-technology-usua.html.

"The Secret to Accelerating Diffusion of Innovation: The 16% Rule Explained." *Innovate or Die.* May 10, 2010. innovateordie.com.au/2010/05/10/the-secret-to-accelerating-diffusion-of-innovation-the-16-rule-explained/.

Andersen, Erika. "The Secret to Getting Really, Really Good at Something." *Forbes*, March 9, 2013. forbes.com/sites/erikaandersen/2013/03/09/the-secret-to-getting-really-really-good-at-something/#827bbbf6588a.

More from

Since 2012, DBCI has been publishing books that inspire and equip educators to be their best. For more information on our DBCI titles or to purchase bulk orders for your school, district, or book study, visit **DaveBurgessconsulting.com/DBCIbooks**.

The EduProtocol Field Guide

by Marlena Hebern and Jon Corippo

More from the *PIRATE*™ Series

Teach Like a PIRATE by Dave Burgess

eXPlore Like a Pirate by Michael Matera

Learn Like a Pirate by Paul Solarz

Play Like a Pirate by Quinn Rollins

Run Like a Pirate by Adam Welcome

Lead Like a PIRATE™ Series

Lead Like a PIRATE by Shelley Burgess and Beth Houf

Balance Like a Pirate by Jessica Cabeen, Jessica Johnson, and Sarah Johnson

Lead beyond Your Title by Nili Bartley

Lead with Culture by Jay Billy

Lead with Literacy by Mandy Ellis

Leadership & School Culture

Culturize by Jimmy Casas
Escaping the School Leader's Dunk Tank by Rebecca Coda and Rick Jetter
From Teacher to Leader by Starr Sackstein
The Innovator's Mindset by George Couros
Kids Deserve It! by Todd Nesloney and Adam Welcome
Let Them Speak by Rebecca Coda and Rick Jetter
The Limitless School by Abe Hege and Adam Dovico
The Pepper Effect by Sean Gaillard
The Principled Principal by Jeffrey Zoul and Anthony McConnell
Relentless by Hamish Brewer
The Secret Solution by Todd Whitaker, Sam Miller, and Ryan Donlan
Start. Right. Now. by Todd Whitaker, Jeffrey Zoul, and Jimmy Casas
Stop. Right. Now. by Jimmy Casas and Jeffrey Zoul
They Call Me "Mr. De" by Frank DeAngelis
Unmapped Potential by Julie Hasson and Missy Lennard
Word Shift by Joy Kirr
Your School Rocks by Ryan McLane and Eric Lowe

Technology & Tools

50 Things You Can Do with Google Classroom by Alice Keeler and Libbi Miller
50 Things to Go Further with Google Classroom by Alice Keeler and Libbi Miller
140 Twitter Tips for Educators by Brad Currie, Billy Krakower, and Scott Rocco
Block Breaker by Brian Aspinall
Code Breaker by Brian Aspinall
Google Apps for Littles by Christine Pinto and Alice Keeler
Master the Media by Julie Smith
Shake Up Learning by Kasey Bell
Social LEADia by Jennifer Casa-Todd
Teaching Math with Google Apps by Alice Keeler and Diana Herrington
Teachingland by Amanda Fox and Mary Ellen Weeks

Teaching Methods & Materials

All 4s and 5s by Andrew Sharos

The Classroom Chef by John Stevens and Matt Vaudrey

Ditch That Homework by Matt Miller and Alice Keeler

Ditch That Textbook by Matt Miller

Don't Ditch That Tech by Matt Miller, Nate Ridgway, and Angelia Ridgway

EDrenaline Rush by John Meehan

Educated by Design by Michael Cohen, The Tech Rabbi

Instant Relevance by Denis Sheeran

LAUNCH by John Spencer and A.J. Juliani

Make Learning MAGICAL by Tisha Richmond

Pure Genius by Don Wettrick

The Revolution by Darren Ellwein and Derek McCoy

Shift This! by Joy Kirr

Spark Learning by Ramsey Musallam

Sparks in the Dark by Travis Crowder and Todd Nesloney

Table Talk Math by John Stevens

The Wild Card by Hope and Wade King

The Writing on the Classroom Wall by Steve Wyborney

Inspiration, Professional Growth, & Personal Development

Be REAL by Tara Martin

Be the One for Kids by Ryan Sheehy

Creatively Productive by Lisa Johnson

The EduNinja Mindset by Jennifer Burdis

Empower Our Girls by Lynmara Colón and Adam Welcome

The Four O'Clock Faculty by Rich Czyz

How Much Water Do We Have? by Pete and Kris Nunweiler

P Is for Pirate by Dave and Shelley Burgess

A Passion for Kindness by Tamara Letter

The Path to Serendipity by Allyson Apsey

Sanctuaries by Dan Tricarico

Shattering the Perfect Teacher Myth by Aaron Hogan
Stories from Webb by Todd Nesloney
Talk to Me by Kim Bearden
Teach Me, Teacher by Jacob Chastain
Through the Lens of Serendipity by Allyson Apsey
The Zen Teacher by Dan Tricarico

Children's Books

Beyond Us by Aaron Polansky
Dolphins in Trees by Aaron Polansky
I Want to Be a Lot by Ashley Savage
The Princes of Serendip by Allyson Apsey
Zom-Be a Design Thinker by Amanda Fox

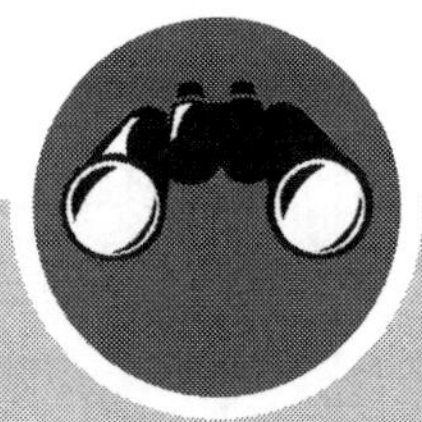

Bring EduProtocols **to Your District**

EduProtocols Workshop

As teachers, how can we focus students on content instead of understanding the task? How can we give more feedback in class and spend less time grading after school? How can we move the Four Cs to the forefront of classroom instruction? In a fun, hands-on, high-energy session, Jon and/or Marlena will share classroom-tested EduProtocols to enhance and reshape classroom learning experiences that will include tons of ideas to be implemented nearly immediately in a school or district. Jon and/or Marlena will customize this hands-on workshop to meet the needs of your school or district.

EduProtocols Keynote

In this fun and engaging keynote, Jon or Marlena will share a new mindset to reimagine classroom instruction through the use of EduProtocols to deliver content to students in fun, engaging, student-centered activities. UDL friendly and Four C rich, EduProtocols span the grades and content areas, and students love them! Marlena or Jon will share some of their stories behind EduProtocols and teachers will leave with new ideas and tips for implementing EduProtocols in their classroom.

Connect with us on Twitter @mhebern and @jcorippo

Visit our website at EduProtocols.com

About the Authors

Marlena Hebern is known for her gentle approach to educators. She draws upon her eighteen years of successful classroom experience when training, supporting, and coaching teachers on engaging students through technology, hands-on tech, and district implementation of technology programs.

After spending summers working at summer camps and as a swimming instructor, Marlena decided to pursue a career in education. Those early outdoor classroom experiences shaped her approach to education as she looked for ways to engage her students with hands-on curriculum. Her greatest passion was teaching young children to read for the first time. (A thrill that will never grow old!)

Marlena also worked as an English language arts K–8 academic coach and as an English Language Arts K–8/English Language Learner Services Coordinator. She especially loves her current job as Coordinator II of Instructional Technology Services at Fresno County Superintendent of Schools in California's Central Valley because she's in classrooms working with educators most of the time!

Marlena has been recognized as a Beginning Teacher Support Provider of the Year and has a master's degree in Reading Instruction. She is also a Google Certified Innovator, Google Certified Trainer, and co-founder of Edcamp Yosemite. Marlena also presents at local and regional conferences.

Marlena enjoys her rural home near Yosemite National Park and the outdoors with her husband, who is a talented (and retired) multimedia/video teacher. They are very proud of their two daughters, who are now embarking on their young careers, one as a Human Geographer and the other as an Aerospace Engineer.

Jon Corippo describes himself as a "formerly disgruntled student." He made it almost all the way through school at a 2.9 GPA. His final three semesters in advertising changed everything, though: Advertising classes were project based. Jon's grades shot to nearly 4.0. Also while at Fresno State, Jon served as a graduate assistant football coach, learning about leadership and teaching at the feet of Jim Sweeney. Jon graduated college with no intention of teaching.

After about seven years in non-educational jobs, Jon's amazing wife persuaded him to try his hand in education: He was hooked after just two days as a long-term sub on an emergency credential.

About twenty years later, Jon had served a decade at the K–8 level, opened a 1:1, project-based learning, Google-based high school, served in two county offices, including as an assistant superintendent and IT director. Jon has been recognized as County Teacher of the Year, a 20 to Watch Educator by the NSBA, and as a finalist in the EdTech Digest Awards. Jon also holds the Apple Distinguished Educator, Google Certified Innovator, and Microsoft Innovative Educator badges.

Jon is very proud of his work with CUE, where he currently serves as the organization's director. His work with CUE includes creating the CUE Rock Star concept of professional development, with a focus on hands-on learning and getting teachers connected via social media. CUE Rock Star Camps now include Admin, TOSA, Teacher and Specialized Editions for core areas. Jon has led the development of the very successful CUE Launch program, and the well-received CUE BOLD Symposium. Under Jon's leadership, CUE professional learning has trained over 30,000 educators in only two years.

Jon lives in Coarsegold, California, near Yosemite, with his wife (a very successful educator), three children, and a random number of free-range chickens.

51017123R00103

Made in the USA
Lexington, KY
31 August 2019